Industrial Sickness in Manipur

About the Authors

Prof. G.P. Prasain is an alumnus of Banaras Hindu University, presently working as Professor and Head in the Department of Commerce, Manipur Central University, Imphal. He has twenty-four years of post graduate teaching experience in Commerce and Management. He has contributed many articles and research papers in referred journals and books of social sciences, apart from presenting a number of papers at various national and international conferences. Prof. Prasain has published four books on Entrepreneurship Development and edited five issues of 'Kangleipak Business Review', a journal published by the Department of Commerce, Manipur University. Prof. Prasain has chaired the Technical Session on Talent Management in Globalised Scenario in the 63rd All India Commerce Conference held in Goa University, Goa in the year 2010. His areas of interest are Human Resource Management and Entrepreneurship Development.

Dr. Elangbam Nixon Singh was earlier working as Lecturer in Commerce at D.M. College of Commerce, Imphal and Assam University, Diphu Campus, Diphu, Assam. Presently, he is working as Associate Professor in the Department of Management, Mizoram Central University, Aizawl. He has contributed many articles and research papers in referred journals and books of social sciences, apart from presenting a number of papers at various national and international conferences. Dr. Nixon has published one book on 'Small Scale Industries and Entrepreneurship' and he is Associate Editor of 'Management Convergence' an International Journal of Management, published by the Department of Management, Mizoram University, Aizawl. His areas of interest are Entrepreneurship, Small Business Management, Finance and Accounting.

Industrial Sickness in Manipur

Causes and Remedies

G.P. Prasain
Elangbam Nixon Singh

CONCEPT PUBLISHING COMPANY Pvt. Ltd,
NEW DELHI-110059

ISBN-13 : 978-81-8069-823-1

First Published 2012

Published and Printed by

Concept Publishing Company Pvt. Ltd.
A/15-16, Commercial Block, Mohan Garden
New Delhi-110059 (India)
T: 25351460, 25351794, *F*: 091-11-25357109
E: publishing@conceptpub.com, W: www.conceptpub.com
Editorial Office: H-13, Bali Nagar, New Delhi-110 015, India.

Cataloging in Publication Data--*Courtesy:* D.K. Agencies (P) Ltd. <docinfo@dkagencies.com>

Prasain, G. P. (Ganga Prasad), 1962-
Industrial sickness in Manipur : causes and remedies / G.P. Prasain, Elangbam Nixon Singh.
p. cm.
Includes bibliographical references (p.) and index.
ISBN 9788180698231

1. Business failures—India—Manipur. 2. Small business—India—Manipur. 3. Small business—Government policy—India—Manipur. 4. Industrialization—India—Manipur. I. Singh, E. Nixon, joint author. II. Title.

DDC 332.75095417 23

Dedicated

to

All the

Indigenous Entrepreneurs of North East

Preface

The small scale industries are the hub of many economic activities in a developing country like India. Small scale industries contribute significantly to social and economic development objectives such as labour absorption, income distribution, rural development, poverty eradication, regional balance and promotion of entrepreneurship. It generates immediate employment opportunities with relatively low investment, promotes more equitable distribution of national income, makes effective mobilization of untapped capital and human skills and leads to dispersal of manufacturing activities all over the state and country, leading to growth of villages, small towns and economically lagging regions. The process, if properly nurtured, can help the entrepreneurial class and boost capital formation as well as growth of industries in the small scale sector in urban and rural areas. It will also pave the way for the growth of right type of entrepreneurship in the country.

Manipur, in fact, is one of the industrially backward states of India. By nature, it is quite different from the rest of the country with regard to topographical features, religio-political compulsion, socio-cultural imperatives, infrastructural bottlenecks, natural resources endowments, etc. The most alarming situation of industrial economy of this State is the high evidence of industrial sickness particularly in small scale industrial sector. But, in spite of having such a high magnitude of sickness in small scale sector which is hindering upon the already weak industrial economy of the state of Manipur, yet there has been no effort from any quarter, whatsoever, to involve a deeper probe into this chronic problem. It is, then, quite obvious that increase in industrial sickness results in human suffering due to loss of employment, wastage of scarce natural resources, blocking huge hard earned investment without any returns and a bad industrial image for the state of Manipur in particular and the nation in general.

Considering the seriousness of the problems of industrial sickness which has vitiated the whole industrial environment the present study on "Industrial Sickness in Manipur: Causes and Remedies" has been undertaken to probe objectively the factors that are responsible for causing industrial sickness in the State of Manipur so that remedies can be searched for these causes in order to have a sound industrial economy in the state.

The present study has been divided into five chapters. The concept of small-scale industries and its relationship with economic development, the emerging trends of small scale industries in Manipur, industrial sickness and objectives of the study and research design are presented in chapter 1. In chapter 2, socio-economic origins of sick units are discussed. Chapter 3 analyzes the different causes of industrial sickness in Manipur. The remedial measures of industrial sickness in Manipur are discussed in chapter IV. The conclusion and suggestions of the whole study are presented in chapter V which is also the last chapter of the study.

We wish to place on record our profound indebtedness to Shri Jarnail Singh, IAS, former Chief Secretary, Government of Manipur for his inspiration, encouragement and technical criticism during the entire course of present research work.

We sincerely offer our thanks to Shri K. Mangi Singh, Director, Planning, Government of Manipur for his invaluable advice, suggestions and innumerable helping criticism throughout the investigation. It was his zeal and enthusiasm which made it possible for us to complete the work in record time.

We are grateful to Th. Munindro Singh, Joint Director, Planning, Government of Manipur for his valuable suggestion and the encouragement to us for the completion of this work. We express our deep sense of gratitude to all those entrepreneurs of Manipur whom we interviewed and who gave us their full co-operation in the collection of various informations related to their industries. Many members of All Manipur Entrepreneurs' Association and All Manipur Trained Entrepreneurs' Union have also helped us for our work.

Numerous friends have helped us in the various stages of this work. We must offer our heartfelt thanks to Prof. S.S. Khanka, National Institute of Financial Management, Faridabad, Haryana, Professor A.K. Mishra, Head, Department of Management, Mizoram University, Aizawl, and faculty members of Department of Commerce, Manipur University, Imphal.

We also like to express our heartfelt gratitude to Shri Ashok Kumar Mittal of Concept Publishing Company Pvt. Ltd., New Delhi for taking keen interest in publishing the book in record time.

Once again, we offer our sincere thanks to all those who gave their valuable time, advice and co-operation in the completion of this work.

Rathjatra
13th July, 2010

Prof. G.P. Prasain
Dr. Elangbam Nixon Singh

Contents

List of Tables

List of Diagrams

Abbreviations

AMEA	:	All Manipur Entrepreneurs' Association
AAIFR	:	Appellate Authority for Industrial and Financial Reconstruction
BIFR	:	Board of Industrial and Financial Reconstruction
CPSU	:	Central Public Sector Undertaking
DIC	:	District Industries Centre
EDP	:	Entrepreneurship Development Programme
FDI	:	Foreign Direct Investment
FI	:	Financial Institutions
ICICI	:	Industrial Credit and Investment Corporation of India
IDBI	:	Industrial Development Bank of India
IFCI	:	Industrial Finance Corporation of India
IRCI	:	Industrial Reconstruction Corporation of India
IT	:	Information Technology
MHHDC	:	Manipur Handloom and Handicraft Development Corporation
NABARD	:	National Bank for Agriculture and Rural Development
NSDP	:	Net State Domestic Product
PSU	:	Public Sector Undertaking
RBI	:	Reserve Bank of India
R and D	:	Research and Development
SBI	:	State Bank of India
SFC	:	State Financial Corporation
SICA	:	Sick Industrial Companies Act
SIDBI	:	Small Industries Development Bank of India
SIDO	:	Small Industries Development Organization
SISI	:	Small Industries Service Institute
SPSU	:	State Public Sector Undertaking
SSI	:	Small Scale Industries
WCTL	:	Working Capital Term Loan

1

Small Scale Industries and Economic Development

1.1 Introduction

An industrial unit is sick when it is not healthy. Sick industrial units are those whose accounts are chronically irregular and customers' complaints are increasingly high. Such units are unable to meet their obligations properly. Sickness in industries is a universal phenomenon. However, defining sickness in terms of industries, whether large or small, is still a tough exercise. There has been no standard definition of industrial sickness. Definitions are based on various norms, such as, generation of income, position of liquidity and insolvency, the amount and period of irregularities etc. Different study groups have attempted to define it, but a generally agreed definition is yet to be evolved. In economic sense, an enterprise is sick if it cannot earn a reasonable return on its capital. In another word, industrial sickness is the situation where the revenues of a unit are insufficient to meet the cost and the average rate of return on investment is less than the cost of capital. And the causes of industrial sickness in the industrial sector including small scale industries are not only many but also differ from region to region and industry to industry; therefore, there is the need to study the causes and find out remedies so as to rehabilitate the ones which are viable in order to avoid unnecessary waste of resources.

In fact, the consequences of industrial sickness extend too many sectors other than the banking sector. The following are some of the adverse effects of industrial sickness:

(i) Industrial sickness caused closure of units thereby increasing unemployment and affecting income generation.
(ii) Consumers are deprived of consumer goods on account of loss of production.
(iii) Loss of revenue to government by way of lesser realization of duties, levies and taxes.
(iv) Financial institutions, banks suffer on account of bad debts and loss of interest. Their recyclable funds get locked up.
(v) Shareholders' earnings go down and other creditors loose their money.

1.2 Definition of Sick SSI unit

An SSI unit should be considered 'Sick' if:

(a) Any of the borrowal accounts of the unit remains sub-standard for more than six months i.e. principal or interest, in respect of any of its borrowal accounts has remained overdue for a period exceeding one year. The requirement of overdue period exceeding one year will remain unchanged even if the present period for classification of an account as sub-standard, is reduced in due course; or
(b) There is erosion in the net worth due to accumulated cash losses to the extent of 50 per cent of its net worth during the previous accounting year; and
(c) The unit has been in commercial production for at least two years. This would enable banks to take action at an early stage for revival of the units. The above definition may be adopted for the purpose of reporting the data for the half-year ending 31st March, while for the purpose of formulating nursing programme; banks

should go by the above definition with immediate effect.

The following (Table 1.1) are some of the important changes brought out in the revised guidelines based on the recommendations of the Working Group on Rehabilitation of Sick SSI units' *vis-à-vis* Existing Guidelines:

Table 1.1: Revised Guidelines of Sickness

New Guidelines	*Existing Guidelines*
1. The definition of a sick SSI unit may be changed as: (a) If any of the borrowal accounts of the unit remains sub-standard for more than six months i.e. principal or interest, in respect of any of its borrowal accounts has remained over-due for a period exceeding one year. The requirement of over-due period exceeding one year will remain unchanged even if the present period for classify-cation of an account as sub-standard is reduced in due course; or (b) There is erosion in the net worth due to accumulated cash losses to the extent of 50 per cent of its net worth during the previous accounting year; and and (c) The unit has been in commercial production for at least 2 years.	An SSI is considered 'sick' when– (i) any of its borrowal accounts has become 'doubtful' advance i.e. principal or interest in respect of its borrowal accounts has remained overdue for a period exceeding 2½ years, and (ii) there is erosion in the net worth due to accumulated cash losses to the extent of 50 per cent or more of its peak net worth during the preceding two accounting years. In the case of tiny / decentralized sector units, the period of relief / concessions and repayment period of restructured debts will be two years and three years respectively. In the existing guidelines there was no mention about providing additional working capital.
2. In the case of tiny /decentralized sector units, the period of reliefs/ concessions and repayment period of restructured debts, have been revised, so as not to exceed five and seven years respectively as in the case of other SSI units. While the other existing norms for grant of reliefs and concessions which can be extended by banks to potentially viable sick SSI units may continue, additional working capital limits may be extended at a rate not	As per the existing guidelines, the banks are expected to take as far as possible, a decision on the viability or otherwise of a unit identified as sick, within a period of three months, from the date of receipt of complete information on the relevant aspects from the management of the unit. Further, the finalization of the nursing programme should be completed within a period of three months from the date of such

exceeding the PLR. (i) Viability of a unit should be decided quickly and made known to the unit and others concerned at the earliest. The rehabilitation package should be fully implemented within six months from the date the unit is declared as 'potentially viable'/'viable'. While identifying and implementing the rehabilitation package, banks/ FIs may be asked to do 'holding operation' for period of six months. This will allow small-scale units to draw funds from the cash credit account at least to the extent of the deposit of sale proceeds during the period of such 'holding operation'. (ii) There is a need for increasing the promoters' contribution towards rehabilitation package from the present limits. It is open to the banks/financial institutions to stipulate a higher promoters' contribution, where warranted. Further, in regard to concessions and reliefs made available to sick units, banks should incorporate, "Right of Recompense" clause in the sanction letter and other documents to the effect that when such units turn the corner and rehabilitation is successfully completed, the sacrifices undertaken by the FIs and banks should be recouped from the units out of their future profits/cash accruals.	such decisions. As regards 'holding operation', it is a new concept/facility, which was not there in the existing guidelines. Promoters' contribution towards rehabilitation may be fixed at a minimum of 10 per cent of the additional long-term requireements under the rehabilitation package in the case of tiny sector units and 20 per cent of such requirements for other units. Banks have been advised to incorporate the "Right of Recompense" clause in cases where the concessions/reliefs were beyond the parameters laid down by RBI.

Source: RBI Reports, 2002.

1.3 Kinds of Sickness

An industrial unit may become sick at different stages due to different causes. The sick industries can be grouped in the following ways (Srivastava and Yadav, 1986):[1]

1. Born sickness
2. Achieved sickness and
3. Sickness thrust on them

Born Sickness

This refers to the sickness of a unit which has become sick right from its inception stage due to various causes which are-

(a) Lack of experience on the part of promoters, wrong selection of the project, faulty project planning, wrong guidance given by the promotional agencies of the government, etc.
(b) Time and cost over runs, delays in commissioning of big projects thereby leading capital shortage, liquidity problems like production costs, etc.
(c) Improper financial management, lack of finance, heavy investment in unproductive capital assets, etc.
(d) Locational problems, technological problems like out-dated machinery, wrong collaboration and, etc.
(e) Wrong feasibility study or no study at all regarding market potentialities, consumer tastes, demand, etc.

Achieved Sickness

This refers to sickness to those industries which fail after operating due to internal causes. Internal causes are also known as endogenous factors. Such sickness arises due to:

(a) Inefficient management of functional areas;
(b) Lack of entrepreneurial skills;
(c) Bad effect of government policies;
(d) Unwarranted expansion and diversion of funds; and
(e) Poor industrial relation and labour unrest, etc.

Sickness Thrust on Them

This is a kind of sickness caused by external factors which are beyond the control of the entrepreneur. Some of these external causes are:

(a) Government policies;
(b) Credit squeeze;
(c) Scarcity of raw-materials;
(d) Lack of adequate transport facilities;
(e) Lack of marketing facilities; and
(f) Shortage of power, etc.

Thus, industrial sickness is caused by either internal or external factors. These factors may independently or jointly act for rendering the industries sick. In small scale industries, all these three types of sickness have been found.

1.4 Signals and Symptoms of Industrial Sickness

> "If the diagnosis is wrong, the medicines would be found ineffective.
> If the diagnosis is delayed, the medicines would be least proactive.
> If the diagnosis is time honoured and right, the medicines would be highly effective"[2]

Sickness does not develop all at once. In most of the cases, it starts within the unit itself. Sick unit starts showing up signals which need to identified and monitored before the unit becomes gravely sick. In the early stages of sickness, the warning signs in several functional areas are termed as signals. An industrial unit tends to show the signs of financial distress starting with short term liquidity problems, revenue losses, and operating losses and overdue of external credit until it reaches a stage where it is overburdened with debt and is unable to mobilise sufficient funds to meet its obligations. The signals gradually merge into symptoms and start affecting the plant performance, capacity utilisation, etc. (Table 1.2).

Table 1.2: Signals and Symptoms of Sickness

Signals of sickness	*Symptoms of sickness*
1. Under-utilisation of installed plant capacity	1. Abnormal delay in filing financial statement
2. High manpower turnover	2. Frequent demand for over-drafts
3. Inability to meet overhead expenses in time	3. Persistent cash shortage
4. Negative variations in operational ratios	4. Accumulation of inventories
5. Bad labour relations	5. Continuous decline in sales
6. Frequent interruptions in production	6. Frequent customer complaints
7. Delay in filing financial statement to bank	7. Absence of motivation
8. Misappropriation in financial statement	8. Frequent failure to get accounts audited
9. Failure to pay interest and instalments	9. No provision for future contingencies
10. Improper inventory management	10. Frequent demand for loans
11. Improper quality control	11. Continuous net loss
12. Decline in technical efficiency	12. Frequent stoppage of production
13. Stagnancy in cash credit account	13. Overvaluation of stock
	14. Non-payment of statutory dues
Approach to sickness	Growth of sickness

1.5 Industrial Sickness in India

Industrial sickness is a worldwide phenomenon. Every country has its own laws to tackle this menace effectively. In India, there were multiple laws and agencies dealing with this problem but they lacked coordinated approach. Therefore, a need was felt to have a legislation which dealt exclusively with the problem and the matters relating thereto. Accordingly, the Sick Industrial Companies (Special Provisions) Act, 1985 (popularly known as SICA) was enacted to make, in the public interest, special provisions with a view to securing the timely detection of sick and potentially sick companies owning industrial undertakings, the speedy determination by a board of experts, of the preventive, ameliorative, remedial and other measures which need to be taken with respect to such companies and the expeditious enforcement of the measures so determined and for matters connected therewith or incidental thereto. Essentially this legislation was enacted to safeguard the economy of the nation and to protect viable sick units. It was aimed at reviving and rehabilitating sick industries; that is to say, to resuscitate, revive and rehabilitate potentially viable industries and to suggest feasible and necessary measures. The law provided for the establishment of Board for Industrial and Financial Reconstruction (BIFR) and Appellate Authority for Industrial and Financial Reconstruction (AAIFR) besides defining the sick unit. According to the Sick Industrial Companies Act (SICA) a sick industrial company is defined as an industrial unit being a company registered for not less than five years which has at the end of financial year accumulated losses equal to or exceeding its entire networth.

Board for Industrial and Financial Reconstruction (BIFR)

In the wake of sickness in the country's industrial climate prevailing in the eighties, the Government of India set up in 1981, a Committee of Experts under the Chairmanship of Shri T. Tiwari to examine the matter and recommend suitable remedies therefore. Based on the recommendations of the Committee, the Government of India enacted a special legislation namely, the Sick Industrial Companies (Special Provisions) Act, 1985 (1 of 1986) commonly known as the SICA.

The main objective of SICA is to determine sickness and expedite the revival of potentially viable units or closure of unviable units (unit herein refers to a Sick Industrial Company). It was expected that by revival, idle investments in sick units will become productive and by closure, the locked up investments in unviable units would get released for productive use elsewhere.

The Sick Industrial Companies (Special Provisions) Act, 1985 (hereinafter called the Act) was enacted with a view to securing the timely detection of sick and potential sick companies owning industrial undertakings, the speedy determination by a body of experts of the preventive, ameliorative, remedial and other measures which need to be taken with respect to such companies and the expeditious enforcement of the measures so determined and for matters connected therewith or incidental thereto.

The Board of experts named the Board for Industrial and Financial Reconstruction (BIFR) was set up in January, 1987 and functional with effect from 15th May, 1987. The Appellate Authority for Industrial and Financial Reconstruction (AAIRFR) was constituted in April 1987. Government companies were brought under the purview of SICA in 1991 when extensive changes were made in the Act including, *inter alia* changes in the criteria for determining industrial sickness.

SICA applies to companies both in public and private sectors owning industrial undertakings:

(a) pertaining to industries specified in the First Schedule to the Industries (Development and Regulation) Act, 1951, (IDR Act) except the industries relating to ships and other vessels drawn by power and;

(b) not being "small scale industrial undertakings or ancillary industrial undertakings" as defined in Section 3(j) of the IDR Act.

(c) the criteria to determine sickness in an industrial company are—(i) the accumulated losses of the company to be equal to or more than its net worth i.e. its paid up capital plus its free reserves, (ii) the company should have completed five years after incorporation under the Companies Act, 1956, (iii) it should have 50 or more workers on any day of the 12 months preceding the end of the financial year with reference to which sickness is claimed, (iv) it should have a factory license.

Genesis of SICA, 1985

- Industrial sickness had started right from the pre-Independence days.
- Government had earlier tried to counter the sickness with some *adhoc* measures.
- Nationalization of Banks and certain other measures provided some temporary relief.

- RBI monitored the industrial sickness.
- A study group came to be known as Tandon Committee was appointed by RBI in 1975.
- In 1976, H.N. Ray Committee was appointed.
- In 1981, Tiwari Committee was appointed to suggest a comprehensive special legislation designed to deal with the problem of sickness laying down its basic objectives and parameters, remedies necessary for revival of sick units.
- The committee submitted its report to the Govt. in September 1983 and suggested the following:
    - Need for a special legislation
    - Need for setting up of exclusive quasi-judicial body.
    - Thus the SICA came into existence in 1985 and BIFR started functioning from 1987.

Objectives of SICA

The objectives of this Act (SICA) as incorporated in its preamble, emphasises the following points:

- The SICA had been enacted in the public interest to deal with the problems of industrial sickness with regard to the crucial sectors where public money is locked up.
- It contains special provisions for timely detection of sick and potentially sick industrial companies, speedy determination and enforcement of preventive, remedial and other measures with respect to such companies.

Those measures are to be taken by a body of experts. The measures are mainly:

(a) Legal
(b) Financial restructuring
(c) Managerial

B.I.F.R: No. of Cases Registered from Year 1987 to 2005—State-wise

S.No.	State	1995	1996	1997	1998	1999	2000	2001	2002	2003	2004	2005	Total
1	Andhra Pradesh	10	8	32	31	48	30	31	30	29	44	13	503
2	Bihar	1	1	2	3	0	1	1	8	3	3	0	50
3	Chhattisgarh	1	2	1	1	1	6	1	2	3	1	0	29
4	Chandigarh	0	0	3	1	2	0	1	2	0	0	0	11
5	Dadra & Nagar Haveli	2	0	0	1	0	1	4	0	0	0	0	10
6	Goa	1	0	1	2	2	2	3	5	3	4	2	30
7	Gujarat	8	14	15	38	32	35	47	57	45	45	23	504
8	Haryana	5	3	13	18	15	10	10	8	8	4	1	146
9	Himachal Pradesh	2	3	3	3	0	3	1	1	1	1	0	48
10	Jammu & Kashmir	0	1	0	0	0	7	0	0	0	0	0	6
11	Jharkhand	1	2	1	1	2	0	4	5	2	1	0	44
12	Kerala	3	3	1	2	5	10	6	15	13	12	9	137
13	Karnataka	6	3	9	18	24	21	14	24	26	18	8	282
14	Madhya Pradesh	7	11	15	21	12	22	18	25	22	11	7	236
15	Maharashtra	12	13	42	82	84	95	119	132	101	91	39	1076
16	Manipur	0	1	1	0	0	1	0	0	0	0	0	3
17	Meghalaya	0	0	0	4	0	0	0	0	0	0	0	4
18	NCT Delhi	1	0	7	23	38	41	42	71	38	45	19	335
19	Nagaland	0	0	0	2	0	0	1	0	0	0	0	4
20	Orissa	2	4	1	7	4	4	1	4	6	2	1	69
21	Pondicherry	1	1	0	1	0	0	2	0	1	1	1	17

(Contd.)

(Contd.)

S.No.	State	1995	1996	1997	1998	1999	2000	2001	2002	2003	2004	2005	Total
22	Punjab	9	4	12	21	24	21	29	21	24	21	12	242
23	Rajasthan	5	3	12	12	10	20	15	21	20	16	10	221
24	Tamil Naou	6	5	29	34	39	51	55	69	42	38	18	521
25	Tripura	0	0	1	0	0	0	0	0	0	0	0	2
26	Uttar Pradesh	14	9	17	19	35	23	25	28	12	12	5	344
27	Uttaranchal	5	2	0	2	3	3	4	5	2	0	0	42
28	West Bengal	13	3	14	21	31	28	26	26	28	29	11	392
29	Assam	0	1	1	2	2	1	3	0	1	0	1	19
	Total	115	97	233	370	413	429	463	559	430	399	180	5327

Source: BIFR.

Commutative Details of Companies Registered as on 31.12.2005 (State-wise)

Eastern Region

State	*No. of companies Regd.*	*Net Worth (Rs crore)*	*Accumulated losses (Rs crore)*	*No. of Workers*
Assam	19	771.58	1728.94	16818
Bihar	50	810.54	1963.71	15689
Chhattisgarh	29	423.94	690.60	3852
Manipur	3	3.45	12.11	192
Meghalaya	4	126.64	154.35	889
Nagaland	4	56.70	194.38	1326
Orissa	69	1003.10	1651.37	28455
Tripura	2	5.95	20.84	1414
West Bengal	392	9164.26	17272.84	615496
Jharkhand	44	1745.53	5181.19	258409
TOTAL	616	14111.69	28870.33	942540

Source: BIFR

Important Provisions of SICA

- Constitution of two quasi-judicial bodies—BIFR and AAIFR and their Benches.
- Procedure of the Board and the Appellate Authority.
- Filing of references under section 15 and criteria of sickness.
- Provision of enquiry under section 16.
- Appointment of Special Directors and OAs under sections 16(4) and 17(3).
- Preparation of sanctioned scheme under sections 17(2), 17(3) and 18(4).
- Provision for monitoring of schemes under section 18(12)
- Rehabilitation by giving financial assistance under section 19.
- Winding up of sick industrial companies under section 20.
- Protection to safeguard the interests of the sick companies under sections 22(1), 22(2), 22(3).

- Provisions for dealing with potential sickness under sections 23, 23(a), 23(b).
- Provision in case of misfeasance under section 24.
- Provision for seeking information and giving information—Central Govt., RBI, FIs State institutions and sick companies and in case of amalgamation other companies.
- Power to seek assistance of MMs and DMs under section 29.
- SICA has overriding provisions under section 32 over other laws except the provisions of FERA, 1973 and the ULCRA, 1976.
- Penalty under section 33 for violation of the Act.

Appellate Authority for Industrial and Financial Reconstruction (AAIFR)

The AAIFR (Appellate Authority) was set up for hearing appeals against the orders of the Board only. Section 14 of SICA, 1985 states that the proceedings before the Board and the Appellate Authority would be deemed to be judicial proceedings and it would be deemed as Civil Court for the purpose of section 195 and Chapter XXVI of Code of Criminal Procedure, 1973 and every proceeding before the court shall be deemed to be judicial proceeding within the meaning of Sections 193 and 228 and for the purpose of section 196 of the Indian Penal Code.

It has, however been the experience that the Act has not proved to be effective up to the desired extent to either check the problem of industrial sickness or find timely solution for restructuring the corporate sector. Many deficiencies were noticed in the operation of SICA, which are as follows:

(a) Restrictive definition of sickness and belated cognizance thereof;
(b) Slow pace of BIFR intervention;
(c) Excessive protection to sick industries under Section 22 of SICA providing for automatic stay of all proceedings;

(d) Necessity of consensus amongst secured creditors before finalisation of revival scheme;
(e) Lack of monitoring of sanctioned revival scheme; and
(f) Delays in the winding up of sick companies.

In 1997, the Government brought forward a Bill namely the Sick Industrial Companies (Special Provisions) Bill, 1997 which sought to repeal the Act of 1985 besides strengthening the mechanism of BIFR by making certain far reaching improvements in the existing law. In a nutshell, that Bill addressed almost all the deficiencies noticed in the working of the SICA. But that Bill lapsed on the dissolution of Lok Sabha.

In view of the problems noticed in BIFR mechanism, Government has been considering various alternatives including repeal of SICA and enacting a separate legislation to address the problems of industrial sickness more effectively.

Accordingly, the Sick Industrial Companies (Special Provisions) Repeal Bill, 2001 was introduced in Lok Sabha on 30th April, 2001.

The Bill to repeal SICA contains the following provisions:

(i) The Bill seeks to repeal SICA;
(ii) BIFR and AAIFR will be dissolved.
(iii) All proceedings pending before BIFR and AAIFR prior to their dissolution shall stand abated.

Another Bill viz., the Companies (Amendment) Bill, 2001 was introduced in the Lok Sabha on 30th April, 2001 with the main objective of facilitating or expediting revival/ rehabilitation of sick companies and protection of workers interests and where necessary, winding up of companies. The Bill seeks to provide for the setting up of a National Company Law Tribunal. The powers and jurisdiction presently being exercised by various bodies viz., Company Law Board, Board for Industrial and Financial Reconstruction (BIFR), Appellate Authority for Industrial and Financial Reconstruction (AAIFR) under SICA and powers of High Courts in relation to winding up of companies are proposed to be consolidated and entrusted to the Tribunal with a view to avoid multiplicity of fora to decide the matters regarding revival/rehabilitation/mergers/ amalgamation or winding up of companies. The Bill was referred to the Standing Committee on Home Affairs which have approved the provisions of the Bill with slight changes and presented their report to the Parliament.

According to information compiled by RBI from scheduled commercial banks, as on March 31, 2001, there were 2,52,947 sick/ weak units consisting of 2,49,630 units in the SSI sector and 3,317 units in the non-SSI sector. Among the 3,317 units, the private sector, public sector and joint/co-operative sector accounted for 2,942 units, 255 units, and 106/14 units, respectively. The total number of sick SSI units has decreased from 3,04,235 units to 2,49,630 units but the number of sick/weak units in the non-SSI sector has increased from 3,164 to 3,317. The total bank credit blocked in sick units has increased from Rs. 23,656 crore (as on March 31, 2000) to Rs. 25,775 crore (as on March 31, 2001). The small scale sector has Rs. 4,506 crore (17.5%) blocked in its units while the non-SSI sector has Rs. 21,270 crore (82.5%). Bank credit blocked in the non-SSI sector in private, public and joint/co-operative units was Rs. 17,705 crore, Rs. 2,986 crore, and Rs. 537 crore/Rs. 42 crore, respectively. Since its inception in May 1987 till the end of December, 2001, BIFR has received 5,192 references under the Sick Industrial Companies (Special Provisions) Act, 1985, (SICA). These references include 262 references from Central and State Public Sector Undertakings (CPSUs and SPSUs). Out of the references received, 3,759 were registered under section 15 of SICA. While 804 references were dismissed as non-maintainable under the Act, 550 rehabilitation schemes, including 22 by AAIFR (Appellate Authority of Industrial and Financial Reconstruction)/ Supreme Court, were sanctioned and 953 companies were recommended to be wound up. 296 companies have been declared "No Longer Sick" and have been discharged from the purview of SICA, on their net worth turning positive, after the implementation of the schemes.

Among the 262 references for public sector undertakings 178 (76 CPSUs and 102 SPSUs) were registered up to December, 2001. Rehabilitation schemes were sanctioned for 16 CPSUs and 22 SPSUs. It was recommended that 20 CPSUs and 27

SPSUs be wound up. 4 CPSUs and 7 SPSUs were declared no longer sick. The gross disposal of cases by BIFR declined from 188 in 1997 to 141 in 1998, however, subsequently, it rose to 179 in 1999 to 385 in 2000. However, the gross disposal of cases was 293 up to December 31, 2001.

The Ministry of Finance furnished the details of cases referred to BIFR (as on 30.06.2002), cases disposed of, and cases pending etc. were as under:

(1) References received

(a) Public Sector		268
(b) Private Sector		5181
	Total	5449

(2) Registration Declined: 1371

(3) Cases under Scrutiny: 55

(4) Reference Registered:

(a) Private Sector		3838
(b) Public Sector		185
	Total	4023

(5) Accumulated Losses: Rs. 80283 crore of all the Registered cases as on 31.07.2002

(6) Year-wise Registration

Year	*Total*
1987	311
1988	298
1989	202
1990	151
1991	155
1992	177
1993	152
1994	193
1995	115
1996	97
1997	233
1998	370
1999	413
2000	429
2001	463
2002	264
Total	4023

(7)	(i) Dismissed as non-maintainable	900
	(ii) Winding up recommended to the concerned High Court	1029
	(iii) Dropped on becoming the net worth positive	41
	(iv) Rehabilitation schemes	555
Approved/Sanctioned		
	(a) Declared no longer sick/Revival	314
	(b) Schmemes sanctioned/Under Revival	241
	Total	2525
(8)	Details of Pending cases	
	(i) Draft Schemes Circulated	77
	(ii) Winding up Notice issue	117
	(iii) Under Inquiry	1151
	(iv) Schemes Failed and Reopened	64
	(v) Pending Cases Remanded by AAIFR	44
	(vi) Stay ordered by Courts	45
	Total	1498
(9)	Age-wise pendency as on 30.06.2002	
	Less than one year	255
	1	370
	2	288
	3	192
	4	157
	5	59
	6	20
	7	15
	8	27
	9	9
	10	24
	11	15
	12	12
	13	20
	14	12
	15	23
	Total	1498

Source: Ministry of Finance, 2002 Reports.

1.6 RBI and Rehabilitation of Sick SMEs

The Reserve Bank of India (April 24, 2008) placed on its website (www.rbi.org.in), the Report of the Working Group on Rehabilitation of Sick SMEs for wider dissemination and comments. Comments on the Report could be sent to the Chief General Manager-in-Charge, Rural Planning and Credit Department, Reserve Bank of India, Central Office, Fort, Mumbai-400001 or could be e-mailed. A Working Group was constituted under the chairmanship of Dr. K.C. Chakrabarty, Chairman and Managing Director, Punjab National Bank to suggest measures for improving credit flow to the SME sector as well as measures for early implementation of rehabilitation/ nursing of sick SME units by examining feasibility of bringing in additional capital through alternative routes, such as, equity participation, venture financing, etc. The Working Group held wide ranging discussions with the stakeholders, namely, industry associations, banks and Government agencies. The Working Group submitted its report on April 17, 2008. The Working Group has given various recommendations/ measures/actions, which need to be taken by banks, NABARD, SIDBI, RBI and State Government for enhancing credit flow to the SME sector as well as for early implementation of rehabilitation/nursing of sick SME units.

Highlights

- As an incentive for proper restructuring package at the time of rehabilitation, necessary support for business restructuring, modernization, expansion, diversification and technological upgradation as may be felt necessary by the lenders may also be encouraged. Support schemes like Credit Linked Capital Subsidy Scheme in case of units in other (than rural) areas, KVIC Margin Money Scheme (for units in rural areas) may be extended for rehabilitation packages also.
- The State Governments should introduce a Single

Window concept for providing relief and concessions to sick Micro and Small Enterprises (MSEs).

- In order to incentive the banks to take rehabilitation measures, the repayment of any additional exposure taken as part of the rehabilitation package should be given priority on the cash flows as well as security as compared to other debt.
- The interest of at least six months after commercial production can be included as a part of the project cost. Sufficient moratorium, say, two years for repayment of the principal should also be given so as to prevent cases of incipient sickness at the commencement of production and help units to establish themselves in the market at the beginning.
- Medium Enterprises should be taken out of the purview of BIFR and the banks given the responsibility of their rehabilitation, more so because only a fraction of the medium enterprises are covered under Sick Industries Companies (Special Provisions) Act, 1985 (SICA) and their rehabilitation done under the supervision of BIFR.
- Raising the limit of Rs. 20 lakhs to Rs. 50 lakhs for Lok Adalats, measures to strengthen the DRT/legal machinery, dedicated Bench for SMEs to expedite the process of recovery, Asset Reconstruction Companies especially for Micro Small and Medium Enterprise (MSME) loans are some other suggestions of the Working Group.

1.7 Small Scale Industry: Concept and Significance

More recently, enhancing small scale industries has been viewed as an effective way of fostering the private sector's contribution to both the growth and the equity objectives of development. Small scale industries are found in existence in every country. They play a key role in the industrialization of developing country. This is because they provide immediate large-scale employment and have a comparatively higher labour-capital ratio, they have a shorter gestation period and relatively smaller markets to be economic, they need lower investments, offer a method of ensuring a more equitable distribution of national income and facilitate an effective mobilization of resources of capital and skill which might otherwise remained unutilized, and they stimulate the growth of industrial entrepreneurship and promote a more diffused pattern of ownership and location.

Small Scale Industries have been given an important place in the framework of Indian planning since beginning both for economic and ideological reasons. Today, India operates the largest and oldest programmes for the development of small scale industries in any developing country. As a matter of fact; small sector has now emerged as a dynamic and vibrant sector for the Indian economy in the recent years.

There is no uniformity in the definition and meaning of small scale industry (SSI) from one country to another and from one time to another in the same country depending upon the pattern and stage of development.

As a result, there are at least 50 different definitions of SSI found and used in 75 countries.[3]

The Fiscal Commission, 1950[4], for the first time, defined a small scale industry as one which is operated mainly with hired labour usually 10 to 50 hands.

In order to promote small scale industries in the country, the Government of India has set up the Central Small Scale Industries Organization and the Small Scale Industries Board in 1954-55. The SSI Board at its first meeting held on January 5th and 6th, 1955, defined Small Scale Industry as a unit employing less than 50 employees, if using power, and less than 100 employees without the use of power and with a capital asset not exceeding Rs. 5 lakhs.

The various changes in the definitions of Small Scale Industry over a period in India is resumed in Table 1.3.

As per the Abid Hussain Committee's recommendations on Small Scale Industries, the Government of India has, in March 1997, further raised investment ceiling to Rs. 3 crore for small scale industries and to Rs. 50 lakhs for tiny units.

Table 1.3: Definitions of Small Scale Industry

Year	Investment Criterion		Employment Criterion
	SSI Unit	*Ancillary Unit*	
Upto 1958	Fixed capital investment up to Rs. 5 lakhs	Same as SSI Unit	Employment up to 50 workers if using power or up to 100 if not using power.
1959	The value of machine was taken as the original price paid irrespective of new or old machinery	Same as SSI Unit	Employment up to 50 workers if using power or up to 100 workers if not using power.
1960	The Gross value of fixed assets up to Rs. 5 lakhs	Gross value of fixed assets up to Rs. 10 lakhs	Employment criterion dropped
1966*	Rs. 7.5 lakhs	Rs. 10 lakhs	Employment criterion dropped
1975	Rs. 10 lakhs	Rs. 15 lakhs	Employment criterion dropped
1980	Rs. 20 lakhs	Rs. 25 lakhs	Employment criterion dropped
1985	Rs. 35 lakhs	Rs. 45 lakhs	Employment criterion dropped
1991	Rs. 60 lakhs	Rs. 75 lakhs	Employment criterion dropped

Source: S.S. Khanka; Growth *vis-à-vis* Sickness in Small Scale Industries in India, *Productivity*, Vol. 35, No. 3, October-December, 1994, pp. 488-493.

Note: Since 1996 investment limit applicable only to plant and machinery.

* The export units are those who export at least 30 per cent of the annual production. The ceiling of investment shall be Rs. 75 lakhs for it.

The new policy initiative in 1999-2000 for the small scale sector has reduced the investment limit for small scale and ancillary undertakings from existing Rs. 3 crore to Rs. 1 crore.

An ancillary unit is one which sells not less than 50 per cent of its products to one or more industrial units.

For small scale industries, the Planning Commission of India uses terms 'village and small scale industries'. These include modern small scale industries and the traditional cottage and household industries.

The "Micro, Small and Medium Enterprises Development Act, 2006" which became operational from October 2, 2006, been changed the earlier concept of 'Industries' to 'Enterprises'. As per this act, enterprises have been classified broadly into:

(1) Enterprises engaged in the manufacture/production of goods pertaining to any industry; and
(2) Enterprises engaged in providing/rendering of services. Manufacturing Enterprises have been defined in terms of investment in plant and machinery (excluding land and buildings) and further classified into:
   (a) Micro Enterprises—investment up to Rs. 25 lakhs;
   (b) Small Enterprises—investment above Rs. 25 lakhs and up to Rs 5. crore;
   (c) Medium Enterprises—investment above Rs. 5 crore and up to Rs. 10 crore.

The Service enterprises have been defined in terms of their investment in equipment (excluding land and buildings) and further classified into:

(a) Micro Enterprises—investment up to Rs. 10 lakhs;
(b) Small Enterprises—investment above Rs. 10 lakhs and up to Rs. 2 crore;
(c) Medium Enterprises—investment above Rs. 2 crore and up to Rs. 5 crore.

It defines 'Medium Enterprises' to facilitate achievement of economies of scale. It provides statutory basis to purchase preference policy for goods and services provided by micro and small enterprises. It also strengthens the legal provisions to check delayed payments to micro and small enterprises. The Act provides statutory basis to the National Board for Micro, Small and Medium Enterprises. The cumbersome two-stage registration process of SSI has been substituted with an optional filing of memorandum by Micro, Small and Medium Enterprises.

The Act aims at facilitating the promotion and development of small and medium enterprises in a competitive way. It seeks to empower the Central Government to notify programmes, guidelines or instructions for facilitating the promotion and growth of small and medium enterprises. One of its primary objectives is to make provisions for ensuring timely and smooth flow of credit to small and medium enterprises.

On the other hand, small scale industries are known and defined with different names and characteristics in different countries. In the USA, the manufacturing firm is officially a small business for Government procurement purposes, if it is not dominant in its field of operations and if it has fewer than 500 employees, or if it is certified as small by the small business administration for purposes fewer than 250 employees, depending on size and the standard set for different industries. In the UK, there is no demarcation between small and large industries. However, in books and treatises on industrial subjects, units employing less than 500 workers are generally referred to as small units.[5]

1.8 Evaluation of Small Scale Industries

The recent years have witnessed a dramatic expansion in the small scale sector in almost all parts of the world. It is not only in developing countries that have experienced such a phenomenon but a similar experience has also been gathered by a large number of industrially developed countries like Japan, U.K., Germany, U.S.A., Switzerland, etc.

Japan for instance, achieved rapid industrialization through the small scale sector in the latter half of the 19th century. The small scale sector in this country plays a catalytic and predominant role in the accelerated growth of the economy.

Even in the developed countries of Western Europe and United States of America, there is recognition that small and rural industries play a significant role in complementing the large industry and in providing opportunities for creative energies of the skilled people. The watch industry in

Switzerland—the largest in the world—is based on the work of a multitude of small, almost cottage industrial units.[6] So important were small firms considered in United Kingdom that a report (Boiton Committee, 1971) paradise the famous saying of Voltaire that. "if small business does not exist, it would be necessary to invent it". In the United States of America, small business administration, more than 30 years old, had been placed on a statutory footing reporting directly to the President.

1.9 Small Scale Industries in India

The small scale industries are the hub of many economic activities in a developing country like India. The role played by these industries in the economic activity of advanced industrialized countries is also very significant. The socio-economic transformation of India cannot be achieved without paying adequate attention to the development of this labour intensive and capital sparing sector.

The most significant aspect of small industry development is that this sector has stimulated economic activity of a far reaching magnitude and has created a sense of confidence among a huge number of small entrepreneurs about their strength and validity. For example, the small scale industries have registered a phenomenal growth in their number, production, employment and exports over the years.[7]

Their numbers have grown from 16000 in 1950 to 31.21 lakhs in 1998-99. While production has registered an increase of more than twenty times, employment grew by about three times over the period 1974-99. Growth in exports has been particularly commendable from mere Rs. 393 crores in 1973-74 to a mounting high figure of Rs. 57,488 crores in 1998-99. It is also encouraging to mention that the small scale enterprises account for 35 per cent of the gross value of the output in the manufacturing sector, about 80 per cent of the total industrial employment and about 40 per cent of the total exports of the country.

The Government of India has also given important emphasis to the development of small scale industries in the country's Five Year Plans. The rationale behind such an approach is that small scale industries provide substantial scope for increasing employment as they are labour intensive and they require comparatively less capital. They have lesser gestation period and can easily be set up in rural areas or in backward areas. They need relatively small markets to be economical and hence they have advantage in being set up as ancillary units. They stimulate growth of entrepreneurship and promote a more decentralized pattern of ownership and location.

Since independence, these industries have made an all round effort to boost the economy. The traditional village and cottage industries provide a vital means of livelihood to village artisans. These industries create the scope of employment to the rural mass and by the way their act as a positive catalyst to ensure the quality of life to the village people. At the same time, these labour intensive industries are considered to be the important means of checking economic concentration in the hands of a few. Equitable distribution of national income is the thrust of our economic policy and towards this end; small scale industries play a crucial role. Employment generation, minimization of economic dispersal, development of backward areas, improvement of the quality of the village population are some of the many important dimensions of our pragmatic planning which always encourages the growth of small scale industries.

1.10 Small Scale Industries and Economic Development

Small scale industries contribute significantly to social and economic development objectives such as labour absorption, income distribution, rural development, poverty eradication, regional balance and promotion of entrepreneurship. It generates immediate employment opportunities with relative low capital/investment, promotes more equitable distribution of national income, makes effective mobilization of untapped capital and human skills and leads to dispersal of manufacturing activities all over the country, leading to growth of villages, small towns and economically lagging regions.[8]

Particularly in developing countries, small labour intensive industries have been favoured basically to create employment opportunities in an economy with abundant unskilled labour even though such industries may not always be supported on grounds of economic efficiency. In addition, a low capital requirement, given an appropriate market environment, is believed to stimulate growth of numerous indigenous industries with wide regional dispersal. This helps to promote balanced growth, more equitable income distribution as well as diversification of the industrial structure which often leads to increased utilization of national resources. The process, if properly nurtured, can help the entrepreneurial class and boost capital formation as well as growth of industries in the small sector in urban and rural areas. Such a process creates the basis for transformation of technology management and paves the way for creative development while sustaining national heritage and skills. It will also pave the way for the growth of right type of entrepreneurship in the country.

Empirical studies have shown that small scale industries are important vehicles for meeting the growth and equity with social justice objectives of developing economics. Achievement of these objectives is seen as desirable in almost all developing countries, though the relative importance of these objectives varies from country to country, depending on the differences in the socio-economic and political complexes. In short, small enterprises sector help in generating large scale employment, wage goods and incomes in a fairly dispersed manner; mobilizing dormant skills and resources enhancing entrepreneurship; energising village economies aiding the process of backward area development and playing an important role in the overall process of industrialization.[9]

1.11 Manipur: Industrial Scenario

Manipur is an industrially backward state. Economic reforms have failed to revive the down trend in industrialization. Manipur has practically no large scale industry which can produce a commodity in a large scale. The few small scale industries that are functioning are also not functioning optimally due to lack of availability of resources and the appropriate environment. The share of manufacturing in real Net State Domestic Product (NSDP) declined from 4.16 per cent in 1980-81 to 3.37 per cent in 1995-96. The growth rate of this sector in the 1990's was insignificant. The share of the tertiary sector started dominating the economy without any significant relationship in the commodity producing sectors of the economy. Private sector employment constituted only 3 per cent of organized sector employment. More than 4 lakhs people are registered in the live register of employment exchanges. Even though International Monetary Fund (IMF) studies categorize this state with 23 lakhs people (2001 census) as one of the fastest growing states in India, its per capita income has persistently fallen short of all India level.[10]

The district-wise number of registered industrial units, employment, investment and production since inception up to 31.3.2005 can be analyzed from the Table. 1.4

It can be observed from Table 1.2 that Imphal West District of Manipur has the largest number of industrial units totally 5185, whereas Imphal East District has the lowest i.e. 137. The other 7 districts of Manipur have units numbering less than 1000 each.

1.12 Manipur: Its Geographical Location

Manipur is a state on the eastern frontier of India, covering an area of 22,327 sq. kms. It is surrounded by Nagaland in the north, Myanmar in the east, Assam in the west and Mizoram in the south. It lies within a rectangle contained by 23.83N and 25.68N latitude and 93.03E and 94.78E longitude.[11] The area is visibly marked by two distinct regional peculiarities. They are the valley and the hills. The valley claims about 15 per cent of the total state area and spreads over an area of 1843 sq.kms. accommodating about 65 per cent of the total population. The density of population in the valley is 628 per sq.km. as per 2001 census. The hill region spreads over an extensive area of 20,513 sq.kms. Its small population representating 35 per cent enjoys about 85 per cent of the total area. The density of population in hill is only 49 per sq.kms. as per 2001 census.

Table 1.4: District-wise No. of the Registered Industrial Units, Employment, Investment & Production since inception upto 31-03-2005

Sl. No	*Name of Districts*	*No. of Units*			*Production*	*Unit*		*Investment*			*Employment*		
		SIDO	*Non-SIDO*	*Total*	*SIDO*	*Non-SIDO*	*Total*	*SIDO*	*Non-SIDO*	*Total*	*SIDO*	*Non-SIDO*	*Total*
1	2	3	4	5	6	7	8	9	10	11	12	13	14
1.	Imphal West	2905	2280	5185	44.27	35.27	79.59	9.72	7.29	17.01	15083	11505	26588
2.	Ukhrul	670	105	775	9.73	2.07	11.80	2.70	0.43	3.13	3931	530	4461
3.	Senapati	242	52	294	2.25	1.63	3.89	0.66	0.26	0.92	1056	252	1308
4.	Churachandpur	425	109	534	3.73	3.39	7.12	1.86	0.33	2.19	2231	1085	3316
5.	Tamenglong	277	208	485	1.07	5.16	6.23	0.31	0.87	1.18	564	1121	1775
6.	Chandel	199	130	329	3.61	1.60	5.21	0.81	0.42	1.23	1157	648	1805
7.	Thoubal	437	133	570	11.08	1.26	12.34	3.16	0.2	3.38	3123	746	3869
8.	Bishnupur	507	175	682	11.21	1.14	12.35	2.32	0.36	2.68	3044	852	3896
9.	Imphal East	117	20	137	4.67	0.43	5.10	1.27	0.05	1.32	666	250	916
	Total	**5779**	**3212**	**8991**	**91.63**	**51.95**	**143.63**	**22.81**	**10.21**	**33.04**	**30855**	**16989**	**47934**

Source: "Nucleus Cell", Directorate of Commerce & Industries, Manipur.

1.13 Population of the State

According to the Census of India 2001, the population of the state of Manipur as on 31st March, 2001 stood at 23,88.634 persons. This represents merely 0.23 per cent of the total population of India which is about 1,027,015,247 persons as per 2001 figures. The population of the state among the different districts according to the Census of India 1991 and 2001 is given in Diagram 1.1 and percentage distribution of population in rural and urban is given in Diagram 1.2.

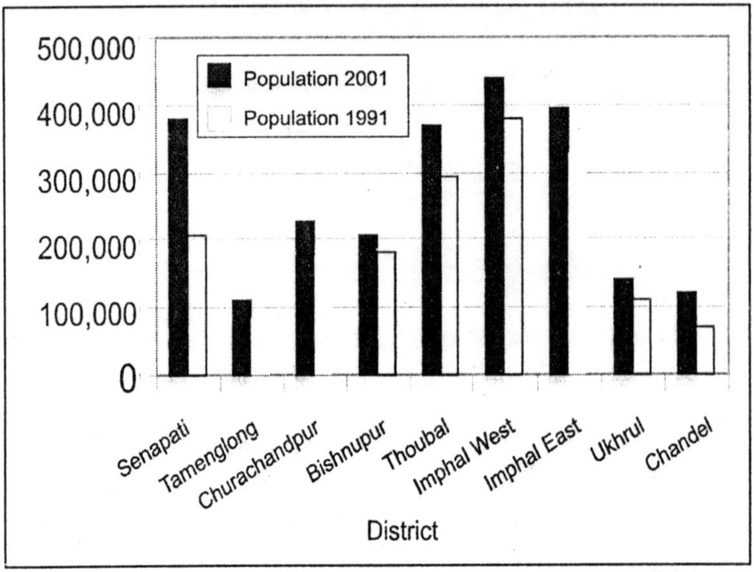

Diagram 1.1: District-wise Population of the State in 1991 and 2001

Source: Census of India, 2001. Population of Manipur, Directorate of Census Operation, Manipur.

1.14 Review of Literature on Industrial Sickness

An attempt is made here to review the existing literature on the subject of industrial sickness. Any literature available on the industrial sickness varies from individual researchers to committee reports, empirical studies to descriptive works and

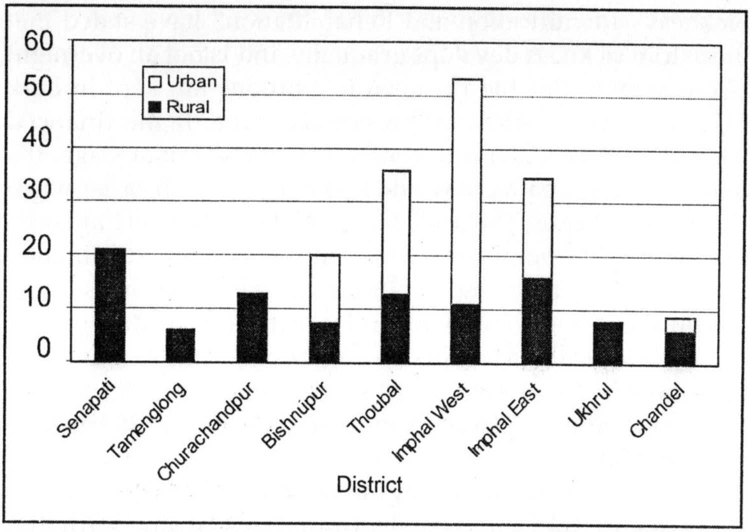

Diagram 1.2: Percentage of Distribution of Population Rural/Urban

Source: Census of India 2001. Population of Manipur, Directorate of Census Operations, Manipur.

general to specific nature of studies. A brief review of literature in this concerned subject is given as follows:

Paul J. Fitz Patrick's[12] study tried to examine whether there was any significant difference in the trend of ratios for failed firms at least three years prior to failure. He concluded that all the failed firms were persistently different from the non-failed firms at least three years prior to failure. It was observed that the ratios of net worth to debts and net profits to new worth were the best indicators of success or failure of the ratios used.

Nalini V. Dave[13] in her Ph.D. thesis in 1987 entitled "Industrial Sickness and Key Area of Management" has examined the strength and weakness of management practices in textiles units against the norms laid down by various authorities of management science. The most significant contribution of her study was that quality to management of the unit is the most important determinant of health of any enterprise.

Bidani and Mitra[14] in their book entitled "Industrial

Sickness—Identification and Rehabilitation" have stated that industrial sickness develops gradually and is not an overnight phenomenon. But the financial institutions are kept in dark till the concern enters into a critical stage. If the financial institutions are taken into confidence at the initial stage, the diagnosis and treatment would certainly be much easier when the problem arises. The book deals with the subject of industrial sickness right from the stage of identification to rehabilitation and follows up the nursed units till they attain normal stature. It emphasises on constant and continuous watch on the transaction in the accounts of borrowers with the banks. In other words, the study conducted by them is concerned with how to tackle the problems of industrial sickness from bankers' point of view.

Mathur[15] made an attempt to identify the major causes of sickness in the small scale industries along with the contributory factors of the entrepreneurs and the commercial banks in the growing incidence of sickness in the small scale industries. His study found that the quality of management of advances by banks to the industrial units plays an important role in preventing the sickness in the small scale sector and in insuring that the units work on sound lines on an on-going basis.

Bhatia and Batra[16] in their book titled "Management of Sick Industries" had collected several papers contributed by experts in the field of industrial sickness. An effort was made in their book, to meet the requirements of Indian industries in managing and monitoring the industrial sickness.

Sahu and Mishra[17] in their book entitled "The Critical Appraisal of Industrial Sickness" thoroughly examined the nature of sickness in Indian industries and outlines a model to predict sickness in Indian corporate sector. The book also presents a clear and systematic approach to understand the symptoms and causes of sickness in industries.

Panda and Meher[18] made a study, which was interdisciplinary in character, exposing the problems of sickness in the SSI sector from multi-dimensional angles. The study took into account both economic and sociological factors that hinder the healthy functioning of the SSI units in an industrially underdeveloped state like Orissa by undertaking intensive field study at one of the oldest and largest industrial estates of Orissa. Factors like improper project planning, entry of unmotivated and inefficient entrepreneurs, lack of demand for the product and infrastructural bottlenecks play a major role in bringing sickness to the concerned units are the major findings of their study.

Singh[19] in his Ph.D. thesis entitled "Industrial Sickness in Manipur—A Case Study of Small Scale Industries" tried to reveal the factors which have actually caused sickness in small scale industries in Manipur. Besides this, the study had accomplished other research objectives like (a) to prevent various conceptual issues of industrial sickness, (b) to highlight the perspective, and (c) the alternate policy measures that have been offered and needed to be taken earnestly to arrest sickness.

Gangwal[20] analysed the causes of 119 sample sick SSI units financed by the Rajasthan state financial corporation and found that the broad reasons of sickness were delay in project implementation, the problems pertaining to the management of the functional areas of production, marketing, finance and personnel and external problems.

Shanmugham[21] studied 50 cases of engineering units in the SSI sector in Coimbatore, started by relatively young entrepreneurs and found that mainly the following problems affected the small entrepreneurs:

(i) Poor financial planning and management.
(ii) Poor collection of receivables (54%).
(iii) Excessive stock level (10%)
(iv) High competition.
(v) Power units.
(vi) Lack of sufficient orders.
(vii) Erratic supply of raw materials, and
(viii) High incidence of sales tax and excise duty.

National Census of Small Scale Industries[22] found that out of the 2,99,186 units registered with the state district industries, as many as 32,315 or 11 per cent were not traceable, another 66,161 or 22 per cent were permanently closed. The closed units were grouped into *five* categories:

(a) Cumulative mortality of units;
(b) Units which have changed their addresses;
(c) Units which were closed down permanently;
(d) Units which could not be located because of incomplete addresses;
(e) Units not in existence and units who have misutilized raw materials and other facilities.

1.15 Need of the Present Study

Manipur, in fact, is one of the industrially backward states of India. By nature, it is quite different from the rest of the country with regard to topological features, religio-political compulsions, socio-cultural imperatives, infrastructural bottlenecks, natural resources endowments, etc. The most alarming situation of industrial economy of this state is the high incidence of industrial sickness, particularly in small scale industries sector. But, inspite of having such a high magnitude of sickness in small scale sector which is hindering upon the already weak industrial economy of the state, yet there has been no effort from any quarter, whatsoever, to involve a deeper probe into this chronic problem. It is, then, quite obvious that increase in industrial sickness results in human suffering due to loss of employment, wastage of scarce natural resources, blocking huge hard earned investment without any returns and a bad industrial image for the state in particular and the nation in general.

The present study tried to analyse the issues of industrial sickness, socio-economic origin of sick units, causes and remedies of sickness etc. Given the seriousness of the problem which has vitiated the whole industrial environment, there is an immense need to evolve a detailed research holistically into the problem of industrial sickness with a purpose to unfold the malady of sickness in small scale industries for framing pragmatic policy implications. The present study *"Industrial Sickness in Manipur – Causes and Remedies"* seeks to probe objectively the factors that are responsible for causing industrial sickness in the state so that remedies can be searched for these causes in order to have a sound industrial economy in the state.

1.16 Objectives

The studies undertaken so far in the field of industrial sickness in Manipur have not highlighted fully the causes of industrial sickness in the state. Hence, the present study has been undertaken with a view to unearth the real factors that are responsible for sickness of modern small scale industries in the state. The study incorporates the following objectives:

(i) To study the overall industrial sickness in Manipur.
(ii) To study the socio-economic origin of sick units in the state.
(iii) To examine the various causes of industrial sickness in the state.
(iv) To suggest suitable remedies for avoiding industrial sickness in the state.

1.17 Research Design

As a matter of fact, industrial sickness in the small scale industries in Manipur is an area of great concern nowadays. With an ever increasing population of the state and less scope for getting jobs in public sector, these small scale industries are the only hope of providing a source of livelihood to the local populace. In these present days of down-sizing and right-sizing in government jobs, a proper study of industrial sickness and finding its measures to stop it will be the only means of empowering the people for economic development.

In the selection of the sample units for the purpose of the study, those with 5 years' existence and not working at present have been taken for study. It had also been ensured to give equal representation to different types of industries and only tnose sick units earlier registered with Industries Department as an SSI have been selected for the study.

The data for the study have been collected mostly from the primary sources. An elaborate questionnaire was prepared for administering among the entrepreneurs. For the purpose of conversing the questionnaire one entrepreneur for each industry has been selected irrespective of the fact that some are partnership firms and some are proprietorship firms.

Apart from these, secondary data has also been collected from different Government Departments like Department of Commerce and Industries, District Industries Centres, Department of Economics and Statistics, Manipur Industrial Development Corporation, etc. The data so collected has been tabulated and analyzed properly with the appropriate statistical tools and techniques.

1.18 Research Questions

1. Entrepreneurship development in Small Scale Industries in Manipur is very slow and far below than the all India average.
2. The Industrial growth in the state has been on low growth path mostly due to more industrial failures in the small scale sector.
3. Lack of demand for products, scarcity of working capital and above all, infrastructure bottlenecks are the main factors for industrial backwardness in Manipur.
4. Improper project planning, lack of industrial conception, absence of entrepreneurial class adoptive to competitive and changing market forces and corrupt bureaucracy has also added to the problem of sickness in small scale industries in Manipur.

1.19 Scope and Limitations of the Study

The researcher faced many constraints in the study in obtaining accurate data from the sampled respondents. The researcher made several visits to the respondents and their units, collected reliable and accurate data. In fact, during this study, the researcher faced many problems which have been overcome to the desired level. The main problem faced was due to the weak data base of the industrial sector in the state, sometimes, it is totally missing. Though elaborate and different questionnaires are designed with simple questions for the entrepreneurs, many of the respondents were not able to respond properly either because of illiteracy and lack of proper records or present law and order problem where everyone is afraid to disclose their financial position in a volatile situation of Manipur.

In short, the study conducted has the following scope and limitations:

(i) The scope of the present study has been confined in the sampled units of nine districts of Manipur. Five sick units each from Imphal East, Thoubal, Bishnupur, Senapati, Tamenglong, Ukhrul, Chandel, Churachandpur Districts and ten sick units from Imphal West District have selected for the present study.

(ii) Field survey was conducted during June-September, 2007.

(iii) As the findings and conclusions of this study are based on data collected from the selected entrepreneurs in the study area, it cannot be generalised for the entire state.

(iv) The methodology followed and tools employed in the analysis of the data involved certain merits as well as demerits of their own and also reflect the limitations of the data base.

(v) All the related data are gathered from the selected entrepreneurs directly. There were no proper records maintained at the individual or firm level. Thus the information given by the sample units may not be accurate. However, utmost care was taken by the researcher to ensure accuracy, by adopting cross checking methods.

(vi) Non-cooperation and unwillingness of the respondents

as well as the government officials and some indifferent attitudes of the concerned officials are also some of the important limitations of the study.

1.20 Presentation of the Study

The study has been presented in five chapters: Chapter I deals with the concept of small scale industries and its relationship with economic development, the emerging trends of small scale industries, industrial sickness, and objectives of the study and research design. Chapter II provides the socio-economic origins of sick units. Chapter III analyses the different causes of industrial sickness in Manipur. The remedies of industrial sickness in Manipur are discussed in Chapter IV which is followed by Chapter V dealing with conclusion and suggestions of the whole study.

References

1. Srivastava, S.S. and Yadav, R.A,: "*Management and Monitoring of Industrial Sickness*", Concept Publishing Co. Pvt. Ltd., New Delhi, 1986, p. 195.
2. Khursheed Ahmed Bhat., "*Modern Small Scale Industries and Industrial Sickness*", Anmol Publications Pvt. Ltd., New Delhi, 2000, p. 21.
3. *An International Compilation of Small Scale Industry,* Definition (Mimeographed), Georgia Institute of Technology Engineering Experimental Station, Atlanta, Georgia, 1955.
4. *Report of the Fiscal Commission,* Government of India, New Delhi, 1950.
5. Desai, Vasant: *Small Scale Industries and Entrepreneurship*" Himalaya Publishing House, Mumbai, 2000, p. 26.
6. P.S. Subbarao: "*Entrepreneurship and Small Business Management*" Discovery Publishing House, New Delhi, 2001, p. 1.
7. S.S Khanka: "*Entrepreneurial Development*"; S. Chand and Company Ltd., New Delhi, 2002, p. 79.
8. Government of India: "*Small Scale Industries in India, Programmes and Institutional Support*", New Delhi, March 1982. pp. 6-7.
9. S.P. Kashyap: "Emerging Industrial Policy Reforms:

Implications for Small Size Enterprises" *Productivity*, Vol. 36, No. 1, April -June, 1995, p. 16.

10. Singh, Nixon E (2007): "*Entrepreneurship in Small Scale Industries in Manipur – A Case Study of Imphal East and West District*", Published by Akansha Publishers, New Delhi, p. 15.
11. S.S. Khanka: "*Entrepreneurial Development*"; S. Chand and Company Ltd. New Delhi, 2002, 79.
12. Yadav, Ram Avatar, "*Financial Ratios and the Prediction of Corporate Failure*", Concept Publishing Co. Pvt. Ltd., New Delhi, 1986, pp. 13-14.
13. Nalini. V. Dave, "*Industrial Sickness and Key Areas of Management*", Deep and Deep Publications, New Delhi, 1987.
14. Bidani S.N. and P.K. Mitra, "*Industrial Sickness – Identification and Rehabilitation*", Vision Books, Delhi, 1982.
15. Mathur, B. Satish: "*Sickness in Small Scale Sector*" Concept Publishing Company Pvt. Ltd., New Delhi, 1999.
16. Bhatia, B.S. and Batra, G.S.: "*Management of Sick Industries*" Deep and Deep Publications, New Delhi. 1997.
17. Sahu, P.K. and Mishra, D.P.: "*The Critical Appraisal of Industrial Sickness*", Kanishka Publishing House, Delhi, 1992.
18. Panda, R.K. and Meher, Raj Kishore: "*Industrial Sickness: A Study of Small Scale Industries*", Ashish Publishing House, New Delhi, 1992.
19. Singh, Tomba Kh. "*Industrial Sickness in Manipur – A Case Study of Small Scale Industries*", an unpublished Ph.D. Thesis submitted to Manipur University, 2002.
20. Subhash Gangwal: "*New Dimensions in Industrial Sickness*", Subline Publications, Jaipur, 1990, p. 115.
21. R. Shanmugham: "Entrepreneurship in Small Scale Industry: A Case Study", *Indian Management*, Vol. 29, Nos. 11 and 12, Nov. and Dec. 1990, pp. 13-15
22. Development Commissioner, Small Scale Industries, "Report on the Census of Small Scale Industries Unit", 1977. Vols. I and II.

2

Socio-Economic Origin of Sick Units

2.1 Introduction

The overall economy of Manipur is agrarian. Even then, the role of secondary and tertiary sector cannot be overlooked in the transition of its economy. Though the economy of Manipur does not possess any basic and key industries of Hirschamanian[1] type to make a breakthrough in initiating economic development, it has a limited number of industries, mostly small scale industries, to initiate the process of industrialization.

Industrialization is one of the important areas for growth and development of economic activities, alleviation of poverty, generation of employment opportunities, removal of regional disparities, etc. Taking consideration of its importance, the state government has been making efforts to bring about rapid industrialization in the state by adopting industrial policies and planned economic programmes. It has been decided to focus attention on the small scale industries and agro-based industries.

But, Manipur still continues to remain as an industrially backward state with all the nine districts under the category of "No Industries District" by all India standards.[2] In view of the economic, political and topographical factors, there had not been any movement worth mentioning for the establishment of medium or large scale industries. The obstacles in the establishment and growth of these industries in the state have been manifold. The long and zig-zag hilly terrains causing transportation problems has been the major constraints for the free flow of raw-materials and finished products. Infrastructural problems like power scarcity, lack of skilled manpower, high production cost, etc. have retarded their establishment in the state.

There were a few medium scale PSUs, but at present, maximum of them were sick and closed down or stopped production as shown on Table 2.1(a). All the other existing industries are small industries, run and operated by private individuals. In 1960, when the development of capital goods industry was given a priority at the national level, the selling up of medium type industry in the state was felt as the logical

Table 2.1(a): List of Corporations in Manipur

Sl. No.	*Name of Corporation*	*Year of Incorporation*
1.	Manipur Agro Industries Corporation Ltd.	1982
2.	Manipur Cement Ltd.	1988
3.	Manipur Cycle Corporation Ltd.	1985*
4.	Manipur Electronics Development Corporation Ltd.	1987
5.	Manipur Film Development Corporation Ltd.	1987
6.	Manipur Handloom and Handicraft Development Corporation Ltd.	1976
7.	Manipur Industrial Development Corporation Ltd.	1969**
8.	Manipur Plantation Crops Corporation Ltd.	1980-81
9.	Manipur Police Housing Corporation Ltd.	1986
10.	Manipur Spinning Mills Corporation Ltd.	1974
11.	Manipur State Road Transport Corporation	1949***
12.	Manipur Tribal Development Corporation Ltd.	1979

Source: Government of Manipur, "An Analysis of the Performance of the State Public Sector Undertakings, 1988-1993" Planning Department, Imphal, May, 1994.

* Incorporated as public Ltd. in 1985, but the company became a Govt. undertaking in 1989.

** Registered under the Companies Act in the year 1969 and upgraded as MANIDCO in 1987.

*** Established in August, 1949 and converted into a Corporation in March, 1976.

necessity for a greater degree of self-reliance and growth. It is encouraging to note that the state government had accepted the responsibility of accelerating the pace of industrial development and after 1970, public sector undertakings were incorporated enmass. This form of management was found effective for dealing with gigantic task of industrializing the state. As a consequence of this, a number of corporations appeared on the industrial scene of the state.

Unfortunately, the return on investment in the state public sector undertakings became increasingly negative from –0.29 per cent in 1988-89 to –31.63 per cent in 1991-92 as shown in Table 2.1(b).

Table 2.1(b): Rate of Return on Investment in PSUs, Manipur

Year	*ROI*
1988-89	0.29% (loss)
1989-90	9.88% (loss)
1990-91	30.88% (loss)
1991-92	31.63% (loss)
1992-93	34.38% (loss)

Source: Government of Manipur, "*Manipur Today*", Directorate of Information and Public Relations, Vol. XVI, No. 1, 26th January, 1996, p. 31.

In the given circumstances, it can be observed that large and medium scale industries are not only few in numbers but also suffered many hardships. There are many problems like:

(i) Scarcity of power,
(ii) Non-availability of raw-materials,
(iii) Lack of proper transport and communication system,
(iv) Poor management of finances resulting in high leverage, delays in lack of synergy and cultural incompatibility.
(v) Wrong personnel policies resulting in overstaffing, poor employee relations, lack of adequate training of employees, and promotion and retention of incompetent managers.

(vi) Authoritarian and conservative attitudes of top management.
(vii) Under political interference in the working of units.
(viii) Technological obsolescence.
(ix) Uncontrolled and non-focused R&D activities.
(x) Poor management of inventories.
(xi) Structural inadequacies.
(xii) Inadequate information system.
(xiii) Conflicts amongst concerned officials.
(xiv) Law and order problems.

Therefore, small scale industry is the only alternative for industrialization in the state. The Government of Manipur in its policy announcement of 1990 has also decided to accord special attention to the small scale and agro-based industries keeping in view the present level of development and the local conditions of the economy coupled with the industrial policy of the Government of India from time to time. It is expected to serve the objective of employment generation and dispersal of industries in rural and backward areas and in this connection, government adopted a policy of encouraging only private entrepreneurs in small scale sector. Various studies on the malaise of industrial sickness in the country have invariably unveiled large number of factors varying from region to region; state to state and industry to industry. Mostly referred factors include poor infrastructure (particularly power), lack of technological upgradation, high taxes, rigid labour laws and inadequate inflow of credit—especially working capital, insistence on collateral securities by banks and SFC, inadequate marketing efforts and facilities, managerial inefficiencies and ineffective delay in settlement of receivables, poor project appraisal, unreasonably short moratorium periods to cover gestation, compounding of interest, high interest rates, poor supervision and monitoring by bank officials, inadequate support and guidance from DIC officials. During our discussion and interaction with the entrepreneurs, we came to know that the major causes of sickness in small scale industries in Manipur are due to non-availability of sufficient funds, raw-materials and electric power; insurgency and other law and order problem and infrastructural problems.

2.2 Profiles of Successful and Unsuccessful Entrepreneurs—A Comparison

All considered, the profiles of successful and unsuccessful entrepreneurs has well served as a list of do's and don'ts, for the benefit of the entrepreneurs, banks and other financial institutions and the government as a whole Table 2.2. Following these patterns, this chapter tried to analyse the selected sick units as well as its entrepreneurs' socio-economic origins. In other words, an attempt is made here to study the district-wise origin as well as the entrepreneurial efforts of the sampled sick units on the basis of field survey, observations, and discussions with the cross-section of people and by referring with different types of publications, papers, etc.

2.3 Year of Commencement of Unit

Table 2.3 shows the year of commencement of the sampled units. 36 per cent of the total units have started their business from the year 1995-2000, followed by 32 per cent in the year 2000-05. Only 12 per cent started commencing their business in the year 1990-1995.

District-wise, 80 per cent of the units in Imphal East District started their units as far back as 1985-90, followed by 30 per cent of Imphal West District. The maximum sampled units of Bishnupur, Senapati, Tamenglong, Ukhrul, Chandel and Churachandpur Districts were newly commenced units as compared to Imphal East, Imphal West and Thoubal Districts. For example, 80 per cent units each of Senapati and Tamenglong Districts were commenced only in the year range 2000-05. Simply put, they can be treated as born sick units.[3]

2.4 Age of Entrepreneurs

As can be seen from Table 2.4, 56 per cent of the total

Table 2.2: Comparative Profile of Successful and Unsuccessful Entrepreneurs

Successful Entrepreneurs	*Unsuccessful Entrepreneurs*
A. Conception Stage (Pre-Project)	
1. While conceiving a project, he is clear about the objectives and the strategies. He is aware of his strengths and does a quick SWOT analysis of the various factors and environments having a bearing on his venture.	1. He conceives a project mostly based on the success of other units in the line, without analysing the factors responsible for their success, and without examining whether the favourable conditions still prevail or the market for the product has already reached a saturation point.
2. Before entering into a venture, he does a quick market survey or market scanning/census to ascertain the extend of existing competition in the market, the demand and supply gap and his own share in the market, on a realistic and conservative basis.	2. Instead of taking such reasonable care, he tends to be over-optimistic, thinking that he would also be able to sell well, as the others in the line are doing, and ultimately lands him in trouble when his products do not pick up well in the market.
3. He has a cautious approach and prefers to learn from the experiences of others who are already in the same or similar line of activity.	3. He tends to be over-confident of himself and ignores to take guidance and advice from the units, operating the line.
4. He is flexible in his approach, examines the suggestions and is even prepared to change the line of his activity if considered necessary.	4. He is rather rigid in his approach and does not seem to be open to reasons and suggestions to suitably modify or scale down his project, or even to switch over to some other line of activity, if necessary.
B. Project Stage	
1. While preparing the project report he proceeds in a systematic way, taking into account the various factors connected with his venture viz. (a) availability of the necessary infrastructure like building, road, power, fuel, etc. (b) availability of the required raw materials, locally or from elsewhere, and whether these would be available in the near future, too.	1. He is over-enthusiastic and impatient to launch his project at the earliest. He does not take due care to examine the various factors, listed alongside in items (a), (b) and (c). His main purpose in preparing the project report seems to be to take maximum finance from bank and the term lending institution. He prefers to do some window-dressing in his project report, depicting a rosy picture about his venture. He is prepare to pay the fees to the professional management

Successful Entrepreneurs	*Unsuccessful Entrepreneurs*
(c) availability of the necessary items of machinery, the names of the manufacturers, their reputation and competitiveness as also whether he should go in for power-operated or hand-operated machines, new or old machines in good condition, depending upon the resources at his command, to begin with etc.	consultants, to prepare the project report on the lines suggested by him, so as to meet the aforesaid objectives, a little realising that it may be even suicidal for the project.
	2. He assesses the cost of the project on a conservative basis and approaches the bank and the term lending institution for further finance, in case of cost overruns, which is usually the case.
2. He assesses the cost of the project on a realistic basis, providing for sufficient margin for cost overruns.	3. He projects his sales and profitability on an over-ambitious scale, which he fails to achieve and starts incurring cash losses, usually from the first year onwards, and tends to fall sick.
3. He estimates the sales and profitability on a conservative basis so as to able to withstand the initial difficulties and set-backs.	4. He usually avoids doing the break-even analysis, or else he does so on an unrealistic basis so as to arrive at a favourable break-even point, for getting the required finance from the bank and other financial institutions.
4. He does the break-even analysis, based on actual and conservative basis, as in items (2) and (3) above.	
5. He may also enlist the services of some management consultant for preparation of the project report, with an open mind.	5. While engaging a management consultant, he asks him to prepare an impressive and favourable project report justifying maximum loans possible.
C. Implementation Stage	
1. He prefers to start the venture on a reasonable scale, which he could manage properly, keeping in view the limitations of his means and resources, experience, expertise, etc.	1. He is over-enthusiastic to start the venture on a larger scale than he can ably manage, to begin with. His main aim seems to be to avail of the maximum credit from banks and other financial institutions, without realising the avoidable interest burden and other risks connected therewith.
2. He tends to go slow and thinks of expansion and diversification only at a later date, after consolidating his positions and gaining sufficient experience and confidence in the line.	2. He wants to grow fast by resorting to diversion of funds for unplanned and non-viable diversifications and expansion, adversely affecting his stability and smooth working.
3. He starts the venture with sufficient stake of his own so as to be able to bear the burnt of the initial shocks as also to have sustained interest and involvement in the venture.	3. He prefers to bring in the minimal capital of his own and is always eager to get his project financed

Successful Entrepreneurs	*Unsuccessful Entrepreneurs*
4. He approaches the bank and other financial institutions for working capital loan and term loans and is satisfied when his genuine credit requirements are fully met by them. He does not press them for over-financing, because he realises that it would unnecessarily increase his interest burden. He knows that when he would start working on sound and profitable lines, they would definitely enhance his credit limits, as and when deservedly required. 5. He adheres to the financial discipline of the bank and other financial institutions, by routing his entire sale proceeds through his cash credit account, maintaining sufficient stocks of inventory charged to the bank, managing his sundry debtors and financial affairs of his unit well, and regularly paying the instalments on his term loan account, timely and thereby building a relationship of mutual trust and confidence with them. 6. After the credit limits are sanctioned, he prefers to withdraw the funds only when required so as to save on account. He also deposits the sale proceeds in his cash credit account promptly to keep the outstanding thereon, and the interest burden therewith, at the minimal level. 7. He avoids overdrawing on his account, except for meeting some emergent commitments, which he pays back fast, at the earliest opportunity, and thereby enhances his creditworthiness and trustworthiness, in the eyes of his bankers. 8. He does not indulge in extravagant and avoidable expenditure and keeps his personal drawings to the minimal	by banks and other financial institutions to the maximum possible extent. This way, he fails to withstand the initial set-backs in his business and tends to lose interest in his venture soon. 4. He is eager to obtain the maximum possible credit from the bank and other financial institutions, well beyond his genuine credit requirements by projecting the estimates and sales at a higher level. This way, his interest burden goes up and profitability is adversely affected. He also resorts to diversions of funds, making the position still worse. He finds himself unable to refund the debt and pay the instalments, with interest, on his term loan, on time. The irregularity on his cash credit account also starts steadily rising. The unit is ultimately declared sick and mostly found non-viable for rehabilitation. 5. He fails to adhere to the financial discipline and resorts to over-drawings on his cash credit account, and does not endeavour to regularise the position. When the bank adopts a firm attitude, he stops routing the sale proceed through his account. His stocks of raw materials and finished goods also start depleting gradually. His sundry debtors are not well-managed making his financial position still worse. He is unable to pay the instalments on his term loan. The unit is ultimately declared sick and mostly found non-viable for rehabilitation. 6. He prefers to withdraw the entire loan amount sanctioned by the bank and term lending institution, unnecessarily fearing the same may not be released to him at a later date. Thus he incurs avoidable interest burden, besides

Successful Entrepreneurs	*Unsuccessful Entrepreneurs*
level of sustenance. 9. He prefers to plough back the profit in the business so that it may continue to expand and grow on sound and profitable lines. 10. He refrain himself from diversion of funds (short-term sources for long term-uses) and unplanned expansion and diversification, because he realises that it would create financial difficulties, adversely affecting the operating cycle and the viability and profitability of his unit. 11. He endeavours to manage the affairs of his unit on sound and profitable lines, and gradually develop professionalism and expertise in various facets of management, like financial management, materials management, production management, marketing management, personnel management, etc. 12. He closely monitors the performance of his unit, on different parameters, on a regular basis, and takes suitable remedial measures promptly so that the unit may continue to work on sound and healthy lines, on an ongoing basis. 13. During the course of his business, he may be confronted with problems and difficulties like scarcity of raw materials, shortage of power, blockage of funds in high sundry debtors, etc. But he does not get discouraged and desperate. Instead, he faces the challenge with firm determination, courage and patience, and ultimately comes out of the wood. 14. His inter-personal relations with his banker and other financial institutions, trade creditors, customers and government officials, are cordial and of mutual	resorting to uneconomic diversion of surplus funds, detrimental to the satisfactory and profitable functioning of his unit. 7. He frequently resorts to over-drawings on his account, on some plea or the other, and neglect to regularise the position. This stiffens the attitude of his bankers towards him, who desists from meeting even his genuine requests in time of need. 8. He makes substantial personal drawings even out of the loan funds, and indulges in extravagant expenditure in travelling, entertainment, etc. 9. By resorting to the aforesaid avoidable expenditure and mismanagement of his unit, he is hardly left with any profit and usually incurs cash losses. 10. He indulges in diversion of funds and unplanned expansion and diversification, in his over-anxiety to grow fast, adversely affecting the profitability and viability of his unit. 11. He lacks the ability, and even inclination, for managing the affairs of his unit on sound and profitable lines which ultimately falls sick, beyond rehabilitation. 12. He fails to monitor the performance of his unit, on a regular basis, and realises his mistakes when it is too late to take the required corrective measures. 13. He loses his heart and confidence when confronted with problems. He tries to shift the blame on to the bank and other agencies, without making sincere efforts to overcome the problems. As his personal stake in the business is usually of a lower level, he ceases to take interest in his unit and allows it to get defunct. 14. Because of his unsound and

Successful Entrepreneurs	*Unsuccessful Entrepreneurs*
respect and trust, which facilitate smooth working of his unit. 15. His industrial relations are also cordial and congenial. He is an effective manager and a dynamic leader. He motivates his people to work well, with devotion and commitment, with a sense of belonging to the organisation and as a well-knit team. This way, the productivity of his unit goes up, and the profitability and prospects therewith. 16. As regards to his personal traits, he is a hard working person, fully committed and devoted to his unit. He works with full involvement for the success and growth of his unit. He is a dynamic personality with passion for excellence. He is an ambitious (not over-ambitious) person and works with zeal to make a mark for himself in the line of his business. He is a man of high integrity and enterprising enough to take fair business risks.	unprofitable working and even dishonest designs and dealings, he ultimately develops strained relationships with his banker and others dealing with him. 15. He lacks the will and skill of managing the various facets of his unit on professional lines, adversely affecting the prosperity and profitability of his unit. 16. He usually starts the venture with the main idea of making a quick buck, at other's cost. He lacks commitment and involvement, patience and perseverance. He lacks courage and confidence to face problems and come out of the difficulties by making sustained efforts. He is over-ambitious and takes high risks initially which lands him in serious trouble, and he usually finds it difficult to come out of it. The risk of his unit falling sick, sooner or later, is usually high and the possibility of its being found viable for rehabilitation rather low, *inter alia*, due to lack of integrity on his part.

entrepreneurs whose units became sick started their units at the age of 31-40 years followed by 34 per cent at the age of 21-30 years. Only 10 per cent started at the age of 41-50 years.

District-wise, Tamenglong, Bishnupur and Ukhrul District had maximum number of sick units that had been started by entrepreneurs in the age group of 31-40 years. Very few started in the age-group of 41-50 years in all the districts. In Imphal East and Imphal West District, majority of them entered entrepreneurship before 40 years of age.

Moreover, the average age of the entrepreneurs hailing from Tamenglong District (33.20 years) conformed nearly to the overall average age (33.24 years), whereas that of Imphal East District (31.60 years) and Imphal West District (32.60 years) entrepreneurs were found to be less than that of the

Table 2.3: District-wise Commencement of Unit

Name of Districts		*Year of commencement of firm* 1985-1990	1990-1995	1995-2000	2000-2005	*Total*
Imphal East	Count	4	1	0	0	5
	% within District	80.0	20.0	.0	.0	100.0
	% within the Year	40.0	16.7	.0	.0	10.0
	% of Total	8.0	2.0	.0	.0	10.0
Imphal West	Count	3	2	4	1	10
	% within District	30.0	20.0	40.0	10.0	100.0
	% within the Year	30.0	33.3	22.2	6.3	20.0
	% of Total	6.0	4.0	8.0	2.0	20.0
Thoubal	Count	0	2	2	1	5
	% within District	.0	40.0	40.0	20.0	100.0
	% within the Year	.0	33.3	11.1	6.3	10.0
	% of Total	.0	4.0	4.0	2.0	10.0
Bishnupur	Count	0	0	3	2	5
	% within District	.0	.0	60.0	40.0	100.0
	% within the Year	.0	.0	16.7	12.5	10.0
	% of Total	.0	.0	6.0	4.0	10.0
Senapati	Count	0	0	1	4	5
	% within District	.0	.0	20.0	80.0	100.0
	% within the Year	.0	.0	5.6	25.0	10.0
	% of Total	.0	.0	2.0	8.0	10.0
Tamenglong	Count	0	1	0	4	5
	% within District	.0	20.0	.0	80.0	100.0
	% within the Year	.0	16.7	.0	25.0	10.0
	% of Total	.0	2.0	.0	8.0	10.0
Ukhrul	Count	1	0	3	1	5
	% within District	20.0	.0	60.0	20.0	100.0
	% within the Year	10.0	.0	16.7	6.3	10.0
	% of Total	2.0	.0	6.0	2.0	10.0
Chandel	Count	1	0	2	2	5
	% within District	20.0	.0	40.0	40.0	100.0
	% within the Year	10.0	.0	11.1	12.5	10.0
	% of Total	2.0	.0	4.0	4.0	10.0
Churachandpur	Count	1	0	3	1	5
	% within District	20.0	.0	60.0	20.0	100.0
	% within the Year	10.0	.0	16.7	6.3	10.0
	% of Total	2.0	.0	6.0	2.0	10.0
Total	Count	10	6	18	16	50
	% within District	20.0	12.0	36.0	32.0	100.0
	% within the Year	100.0	100.0	100.0	100.0	100.0
	% of Total	20.0	12.0	36.0	32.0	100.0

Source: Field Survey.

Table 2.4: District-wise Age of Entrepreneurs at the Commencement of Unit

Name of Districts		*Age of entrepreneurs*			*Total*
		21-30 yrs.	*31-40 yrs.*	*41-50 yrs.*	
Imphal East	Count	2	2	1	5
	% within District	40.0	40.0	20.0	100.0
	% within Age	11.8	7.1	20.0	10.0
	% of Total	4.0	4.0	2.0	10.0
Imphal West	Count	4	5	1	10
	% within District	40.0	50.0	10.0	100.0
	% within Age	23.5	17.9	20.0	10.0
	% of Total	8.0	10.0	2.0	10.0
Thoubal	Count	2	3	0	5
	% within District	40.0	60.0	.0	100.0
	% within Age	11.8	10.7	.0	10.0
	% of Total	4.0	6.0	.0	10.0
Bishnupur	Count	1	4	0	5
	% within District	20.0	80.0	.0	100.0
	% within Age	5.9	14.3	.0	10.0
	% of Total	2.0	8.0	.0	10.0
Senapati	Count	2	2	1	5
	% within District	40.0	40.0	20.0	100.0
	% within Age	11.8	7.1	20.0	10.0
	% of Total	4.0	4.0	2.0	10.0
Tamenglong	Count	1	4	0	5
	% within District	20.0	80.0	.0	100.0
	% within Age	5.9	14.3	.0	10.0
	% of Total	2.0	8.0	.0	10.0
Ukhrul	Count	2	3	0	5
	% within District	40.0	60.0	.0	100.0
	% within Age	11.8	10.7	.0	10.0
	% of Total	4.0	6.0	.0	10.0
Chandel	Count	2	2	1	5
	% within District	40.0	40.0	20.0	100.0
	% within Age	11.8	7.1	20.0	10.0
	% of Total	4.0	4.0	2.0	10.0
Churachandpur	Count	1	3	1	5
	% within District	20.0	60.0	20.0	100.0
	% within Age	5.9	10.7	20.0	10.0
	% of Total	2.0	6.0	2.0	10.0
Total	Count	17	28	5	50
	% within District	34.0	56.0	100.0	100.0
	% within Age	100.0	100.0	10.0	100.0
	% of Total	34.0	56.0	10.0	100.0

Source: Field Survey.

overall average ages. It is quite interesting to note that the average ages of all other districts are found to be more than that of the overall average age.

2.5 Form of Organisation

An attempt is made here to analyse the different forms of organizations started by the sampled entrepreneurs. As can be seen, Table 2.5 highlighted that maximum of the sampled units are proprietorship form of organization (80.0%), followed by partnership firms (12.0%). Among the districts, Churachandpur, Senapati, Bishnupur and Imphal East Districts had only the proprietorship form of organization in the sampled unit. Age-wise, it is very noteworthy to mention that the average age of entrepreneurs who started proprietorship form of organisation are less (33.09 years) than that who started partnership form of organisation (34.33 years). It can be, thus, concluded that proprietorship form of organization is the most common form of organization in the state.

2.6 Type of Industries

Maximum of the sampled units are food based industries (26.0%), followed by metal based (16.0%) and handlooms and handicrafts and automobile and engineering units (14.0% each). As can be seen from Table 2.6, the food based industries sampled are mostly concentrated in Imphal West district (23.1%), Thoubal, Bishnupur and Ukhrul Districts (15.4% each). As far as metal based industries are concerned, they are evenly distributed in all the districts except in Imphal East District. It is quite interesting to note that there are no sick handlooms and handicrafts industries in Imphal West, Ukhrul and Churachandpur Districts as far as the sampled units are concerned.

Table 2.5: District-wise Form of Organisation

Name of Districts		Form of ownership		Total
		Proprietorship	Partnership	
Imphal East	Count	5	0	5
	% within District	100.0	.0	100.0
	% within Form of ownership	11.4	.0	100.0
	% of Total	10.0	.0	10.0
Imphal West	Count	8	2	10
	% within District	80.0	20.0	100.0
	% within Form of ownership	18.2	33.3	20.0
	% of Total	16.0	4.0	20.0
Thoubal	Count	4	1	5
	% within District	80.0	20.0	100.0
	% within Form of ownership	9.1	16.7	10.0
	% of Total	8.0	2.0	10.0
Bishnupur	Count	5	0	5
	% within District	100.0	.0	100.0
	% within Form of ownership	11.4	.0	10.0
	% of Total	10.0	.0	10.0
Senapati	Count	5	0	5
	% within District	100.0	.0	100.0
	% within Form of ownership	11.4	.0	10.0
	% of Total	10.0	.0	10.0
Tamenglong	Count	4	1	5
	% within District	80.0	20.0	100.0
	% within Form of ownership	9.1	16.7	10.0
	% of Total	8.0	2.0	10.0
Ukhrul	Count	4	1	5
	% within District	80.0	20.0	100.0
	% within Form of ownership	9.1	16.7	10.0
	% of Total	8.0	2.0	10.0
Chandel	Count	4	1	5
	% within District	80.0	20.0	100.0
	% within Form of ownership	9.1	16.7	10.0
	% of Total	8.0	2.0	10.0
Churachandpur	Count	5	0	5
	% within District	100.0	.0	100.0
	% within Form of ownership	11.4	.0	10.0
	% of Total	10.0	.0	10.0
Total	Count	44	6	50
	% within District	88.0	12.0	100.0
	% within Form of ownership	100.0	100.0	100.0
	% of Total	88.0	12.0	100.0

Source: Field Survey.

Table 2.6: District-wise Type of Industry

Name of Districts		*Type of Industry*								
		Food based	*Metal based*	*Handlooms & handicrafts*	*Plastics and rubber based*	*Wood based*	*Printing & stationery*	*Automobile and engineering*	*Others*	*Total*
Imphal East	Count	1	0	1	1	.0	0	1	1	5
	% within District.	20.0	.0	20.0	20.0	.0	.0	20.0	20.0	100.0
	% within Industry	7.7	.0	14.3	25.0	.0	.0	14.3	50.0	10.0
	% of Total	2.0	.0	2.0	2.0	.0	.0	2.0	2.0	10.0
Imphal West	Count	3	1	0	1	1	1	2	1	10
	% within District.	30.0	10.0	.0	10.0	10.0	10.0	20.0	10.0	100.0
	% within Industry	23.1	12.5	.0	25.0	20.0	25.0	28.6	50.0	20.0
	% of Total	6.0	2.0	.0	2.0	2.0	2.0	4.0	2.0	20.0
Thoubal	Count	2	1	1	0	1	0	0	0	5
	% within District.	40.0	20.0	20.0	.0	20.0	.0	.0	.0	100.0
	% within Industry	15.4	12.5	14.3	.0	20.0	.0	.0	.0	10.0
	% of Total	4.0	2.0	2.0	.0	2.0	.0	.0	.0	10.0
Bishnupur	Count	2	1	1	0	0	1	0	0	5
	% within District.	40.0	20.0	20.0	.0	.0	20.0	.0	.0	100.0
	% within Industry	15.4	12.5	14.3	.0	.0	25.0	.0	.0	10.0
	% of Total	4.0	2.0	2.0	.0	.0	2.0	.0	.0	10.0

(*Contd.*)

Table 2.6 (*Contd.*)

Senapati	Count	0	1	1	0	1	0	2	0	5
	% within District.	.0	20.0	20.0	.0	20.0	.0	40.0	.0	100.0
	% within Industry	.0	12.5	14.3	.0	20.0	.0	28.6	.0	10.0
	% of Total	.0	2.0	2.0	.0	2.0	.0	4.0	.0	10.0
Tamenglong	Count	1	1	1	0	2	0	0	0	5
	% within District.	20.0	20.0	20.0	.0	40.0	.0	.0	.0	100.0
	% within Industry	7.7	12.5	14.3	.0	40.0	.0	.0	.0	10.0
	% of Total	2.0	2.0	2.0	.0	4.0	.0	.0	.0	10.0
Ukhrul	Count	2	1	0	1	0	0	1	0	5
	% within District.	40.0	20.0	.0	20.0	.0	.0	20.0	.0	100.0
	% within Industry	15.4	12.5	.0	25.0	.0	.0	14.3	.0	10.0
	% of Total	4.0	2.0	.0	2.0	.0	.0	2.0	.0	10.0
Chandel	Count	1	1	2	0	0	1	0	0	5
	% within District.	20.0o	20.0	40.0	.0	.0	20.0	.0	.0	100.0
	% within Industry	7.7	12.5	28.6	.0	.0	25.0	.0	.0	10.0
	% of Total	2.0	2.0	4.0	.0	.0	2.0	.0	.0	10.0
Churachandpur	Count	1	1	0	1	0	1	1	0	5
	% within District.	20.0	20.0	.0	20.0	.0	20.0	20.0	.0	100.0
	% within Industry	7.7	12.5	.0	25.0	.0	25.0	14.3	.0	10.0
	% of Total	2.0	2.0	.0	2.0	.0	2.0	2.0	.0	10.0
Total	Count	13	8	7	4	5	4	7	2	50
	% within District	26.0	16.0	14.0	8.0	10.0	8.0	14.0	4.0	100.0
	% within Industry	100.0	100.0	100.0	100.0	100.0	100.0	100.0	100.0	100.0
	% of Total	26.0	16.0	14.0	8.0	10.0	8.0	14.0	9.0	100.0

2.7 Educational Background of Entrepreneurs

Educational background of the entrepreneurs also plays an important role in the success or failure of a unit. As such, an analysis is made here to find out the educational qualification of the entrepreneurs whose units have become sick.

Table 2.7 shows that 26 per cent each of under-matriculation, under-graduation and graduation formed the number of such entrepreneur. Matriculation formed 20 per cent whereas it is worthwhile to mention that post-graduation formed only 2 per cent.

Among the districts, entrepreneurs who were not matriculates are found in all the districts except in Imphal East and Imphal West Districts. The only post-graduated entrepreneurs were found in Imphal West District. Again, the maximum of graduated entrepreneurs are found in the Imphal West District (42.6%). It is also interesting to note that 80 per cent of Imphal East District entrepreneurs were educated up to under-graduation.

2.8 Professional Experience of Entrepreneurs

Professional experience of the entrepreneurs can also play an important role in the process of industrial sickness. But, it is very encouraging on the part of the sampled sick units that 70 per cent of the concerned entrepreneurs had the unit related professional experience (Table 2.8).

Even among the nine districts of the State, the majority of them had the required professional experience. It is worthwhile to mention that all the entrepreneurs of Imphal East District had experience as far as the type of industry they had started is concerned. With all the required professional experience, now the question is how come their units became sick? This will be an interesting topic in the latter chapter, which relates to causes of industrial sickness.

Table 2.7: Districts-wise Educational Qualification of Entrepreneurs

Name of Districts		*Qualification of entrepreneurs*					
		Under matric	*Matric*	*Under graduate*	*Graduate*	*Post graduate*	*Total*
Imphal East	Count	0	0	4	1	0	5
	% within District	0	0	80.0	20.0	0	100.0
	% within Qualification	0	0	30.8	7.7	0	10.0
	% of Total	0	0	8.0	2.0	0	10.0
Imphal West	Count	0	1	2	6	1	10
	% within District	0	10.0	20.0	60.0	10.0	100.0
	% within Qualification	0	10.0	15.4	46.2	100.0	10.0
	% of Total	0	2.0	4.0	12.0	2.0	10.0
Thoubal	Count	1	1	2	1	0	5
	% within District	20.0	20.0	40.0	20.0	.0	100.0
	% within Qualification	7.7	10.0	15.4	7.7	.0	10.0
	% of Total	2.0	2.0	4.0	2.0	.0	10.0
Bishnupur	Count	2	1	1	1	0	5
	% within District	20.0	20.0	20.0	20.0	.0	100.0
	% within Qualification	15.4	10.0	7.7	7.7	.0	10.0
	% of Total	4.0	2.0	2.0	2.0	.0	10.0
Senapati	Count	3	1	1	1	0	5
	% within District	40.0	20.0	20.0	20.0	.0	100.0
	% within Qualification	15.4	10.0	7.7	7.7	.0	10.0
	% of Total	4.0	2.0	2.0	2.0	.0	10.0
Tamenglong	Count	2	1	1	1	0	5
	% within District	40.0	20.0	20.0	20.0	.0	100.0
	% within Qualification	15.4	10.0	7.7	7.7	.0	10.0
	% of Total	4.0	2.0	2.0	2.0	.0	10.0
Ukhrul	Count	2	1	1	0	0	5
	% within District	40.0	20.0	20.0	.0	.0	100.0
	% within Qualification	15.4	10.0	7.7	.0	.0	10.0
	% of Total	4.0	2.0	2.0	.0	.0	10.0
Chandel	Count	2	1	1	1	0	5
	% within District	40.0	20.0	20.0	20.0	.0	100.0
	% within Qualification	15.4	10.0	7.7	7.7	.0	10.0
	% of Total	4.0	2.0	2.0	2.0	.0	10.0
Chura-chandpur	Count	1	2	1	1	0	5
	% within District	20.0	40.0	20.0	20.0	.0	100.0
	% within Qualification	7.7	20.0	7.7	7.7	.0	10.0
	% of Total	2.0	4.0	2.0	2.0	.0	10.0
Total	Count	13	10	13	13	10	50
	% within District	26.0	20.0	26.0	26.0	2.0	100.0
	% within Qualification	100.0	100.0	100.0	100.0	100.0	100.0
	% of Total	26.0	20.0	26.0	26.0	2.0	100.0

Source: Field Survey.

Table 2.8: Districts-wise Professional Experience of Entrepreneurs

Name of Districts		*Professional experience*		*Total*
		Yes	*No*	
Imphal East	Count	5	0	5
	% within District	100.0	.0	100.0
	% within Professional experience	14.3	.0	14.3
	% of Total	10.0	.0	10.0
Imphal West	Count	8	2	10
	% within District	80.0	20.0	100.0
	% within Professional experience	22.9	13.3	20.0
	% of Total	16.0	4.0	20.0
Thoubal	Count	3	2	5
	% within District	60.0	40.0	100.0
	% within Professional experience	8.6	13.3	10.0
	% of Total	6.0	4.0	10.0
Bishnupur	Count	3	2	5
	% within District	60.0	40.0	100.0
	% within Professional experience	8.6	13.3	10.0
	% of Total	6.0	4.0	10.0
Senapati	Count	3	2	5
	% within District	60.0	40.0	100.0
	% within Professional experience	8.6	13.3	10.0
	% of Total	6.0	4.0	10.0
Tamenglong	Count	3	2	5
	% within District	60.0	40.0	100.0
	% within Professional experience	8.6	13.3	10.0
	% of Total	6.0	4.0	10.0
Ukhrul	Count	3	2	5
	% within District	60.0	40.0	100.0
	% within Professional experience	8.6	13.3	10.0
	% of Total	6.0	4.0	10.0
Chandel	Count	3	2	5
	% within District	60.0	40.0	100.0
	% within Professional experience	8.6	13.3	10.0
	% of Total	6.0	4.0	10.0
Churachandpur	Count	4	1	5
	% within District	80.0	20.0	100.0
	% within Professional experience	11.4	6.7	10.0
	% of Total	8.0	2.0	10.0
Total	Count	35	15	50
	% within District	70.0	30.0	100.0
	% within Professional experience	100.0	100.0	100.0
	% of Total	70.0	30.0	100.0

Source: Field Survey.

2.9 Generation of Entrepreneurs

Here, an attempt is made to analyse the entrepreneurs on the basis of their generation. Table 2.9 notes that 78 per cent of the total sampled entrepreneurs are first generation interpreters. Further, entrepreneurs hailing from Imphal East, Bishnupur and Chandel Districts are all first generation entrepreneurs. Quite interestingly, 60 per cent of Tamenglong District is second generation entrepreneurs. Again, it can be noted that there is no third generation entrepreneurs among the sampled units.

Thus, it can be concluded that even though maximum of the entrepreneurs had professional experience in their related field, they are fresh in their own practical field of entrepreneurship.

2.10 Feasibility Study

Feasibility studies tries to find and analyse the viability of the unit in the coming days to come. It is generally undertaken before the commencement of the business or production. Table 2.10 shows the feasibility study undertaken by sampled units.

As can be seen, out of the total 50 entrepreneurs, only 21 (42.0%) conducted the feasibility study before commencement of their units. Quite surprisingly, none of the Thoubal and Senapati District entrepreneurs had conducted any sort of feasibility study. The same pattern continues in the case of Bishnupur, Tamenglong, Ukhrul and Chandel District where maximum of the sampled entrepreneurs didn't conduct the study (more than 60.0%). It is very interesting to note that, in case of Imphal East District, all of the entrepreneurs had undertaken the feasibility study.

After analysing whether the sampled entrepreneurs had or had not undertaken any feasibility study. Table 2.11 tries to find out how the 21 entrepreneurs had conducted the feasibility study. As can be seen, 8 out of 21 (38.1%) conducted the study by themselves whereas the remaining 13 took the help of other agencies like SBI, SISI, AMEA, DIC, etc. for conducting the said study.

Table 2.9: Districts-wise Generation of Entrepreneurs

Name of Districts		*Generation*		*Total*
		First Generation	*Second Generation*	
Imphal East	Count	5	.0	5
	% within District	100.0	.0	100.0
	% within Generation	12.8	.0	10.0
	% of Total	10.0	.0	10.0
Imphal West	Count	8	2	10
	% within District	80.0	20.0	100.0
	% within Generation	20.5	18.2	20.0
	% of Total	16.0	4.0	20.0
Thoubal	Count	4	1	5
	% within District	80.0	20.0	100.0
	% within Generation	10.3	9.1	10.0
	% of Total	8.0	2.0	10.0
Bishnupur	Count	5	.0	5
	% within District	100.0	.0	100.0
	% within Generation	12.8	.0	10.0
	% of Total	10.0	.0	10.0
Senapati	Count	3	2	5
	% within District	60.0	40.0	100.0
	% within Generation	7.7	18.2	10.0
	% of Total	6.0	4.0	10.0
Tamenglong	Count	2	3	5
	% within District	40.0	60.0	100.0
	% within Generation	5.1	27.3	10.0
	% of Total	4.0	6.0	10.0
Ukhrul	Count	3	2	5
	% within District	60.0	40.0	100.0
	% within Generation	7.7	18.2	10.0
	% of Total	6.0	4.0	10.0
Chandel	Count	5	.0	5
	% within District	100.0	.0	100.0
	% within Generation	12.8	.0	10.0
	% of Total	10.0	.0	10.0
Churachandpur	Count	4	1	5
	% within District	80.0	20.0	100.0
	% within Generation	10.3	9.1	10.0
	% of Total	8.0	2.0	10.0
Total	Count	39	11	50
	% within District	78.0	22.0	100.0
	% within Generation	100.0	100.0	100.0
	% of Total	78.0	22.0	100.0

Source: Field Survey.

Table 2.10: District-wise Feasibility Study

Name of Districts		*Feasibility study*		*Total*
		Yes	*No*	
Imphal East	Count	5	0	5
	% within District	100.0	0	100.0
	% within Feasibility study	23.8	0	10.0
	% of Total	10.0	0	10.0
Imphal West	Count	6	4	10
	% within District	60.0	40.0	100.0
	% within Feasibility study	28.6	13.8	10.0
	% of Total	12.0	8.0	10.0
Thoubal	Count	0	5	5
	% within District	0	100.0	100.0
	% within Feasibility study	0	17.2	10.0
	% of Total	0	10.0	10.0
Bishnupur	Count	2	3	5
	% within District	40.0	60.0	100.0
	% within Feasibility study	9.5	10.3	10.0
	% of Total	4.0	6.0	10.0
Senapati	Count	0	5	5
	% within District	0	100.0	100.0
	% within Feasibility study	0	17.2	10.0
	% of Total	0	10.0	10.0
Tamenglong	Count	1	4	5
	% within District	20.0	80.0	100.0
	% within Feasibility study	4.8	13.8	10.0
	% of Total	2.0	8.0	10.0
Ukhrul	Count	2	3	5
	% within District	40.0	60.0	100.0
	% within Feasibility study	9.5	10.0	10.0
	% of Total	4.0	6.0	10.0
Chandel	Count	2	3	5
	% within District	40.0	60.0	100.0
	% within Feasibility study	9.5	10.3	10.0
	% of Total	4.0	6.0	10.0
Churachandpur	Count	3	2	5
	% within District	60.0	40.0	100.0
	% within Feasibility study	14.3	6.9	10.0
	% of Total	6.0	4.0	10.0
Total	Count	21	29	50
	% within District	42.0	58.0	100.0
	% within Feasibility study	100.0	100.0	100.0
	% of Total	42.0	58.0	100.0

Source: Field Survey.

Table 2.11: Mode of Conducting Feasibility Study

Name of Districts		*Feasibility Study*		*Total*
		Conducted by Self	*Conducted through other agencies*	
Imphal East	Count	0	5	5
	% within District	0	100.0	100.0
	% within Feasibility Study	0	38.5	23.8
	% of Total	0	23.8	23.8
Imphal West	Count	3	3	6
	% within District	50.0	50.0	100.0
	% within Feasibility Study	37.5	23.1	28.6
	% of Total	14.3	14.3	28.6
Bishnupur	Count	2	0	2
	% within District	100.0	0	100.0
	% within Feasibility Study	25.0	0	9.5
	% of Total	9.5	0	9.5
Tamenglong	Count	0	1	1
	% within District	0	100.0	100.0
	% within Feasibility Study	0	7.7	4.8
	% of Total	0	4.8	4.8
Ukhrul	Count	1	1	2
	% within District	50.0	50.0	100.0
	% within Feasibility Study	12.5	7.7	9.5
	% of Total	4.8	4.8	9.5
Chandel	Count	0	2	2
	% within District	0	100.0	100.0
	% within Feasibility Study	0	15.4	9.5
	% of Total	0	9.5	9.5
Churachandpur	Count	2	1	3
	% within District	66.7	33.3	100.0
	% within Feasibility Study	25.0	7.7	14.3
	% of Total	9.5	4.8	14.3
Total	Count	8	13	21
	% within District	38.1	61.9	100.0
	% within Feasibility Study	100.0	100.0	100.0
	% of Total	38.1	61.9	100.0

Source: Field Survey.

District-wise also, entrepreneurs hailing from Imphal East, Tamenglong, Chandel had entrusted the job of conducting the feasibility study with other experienced body. It can also be noted that all the entrepreneurs who had undertaken feasibility study in Thoubal District believed in themselves as far as the study was concerned.

It can thus be concluded that maximum of those who had conducted the feasibility study had taken it through other agencies.

2.11 Entrepreneurship Development Programme (EDP)

To ascertain whether the sampled entrepreneurs had any entrepreneurial traits, Table 2.12 shows the district-wise attendance of EDP by them. As can be seen, 26 (52.0%) of the total 50 entrepreneurs attended EDP, conducted by various agencies. District-wise, Imphal West District had the maximum number of such entrepreneurs (16.0%) followed by Imphal East District (10.0%) and Churachandpur District (6.0%).

It is worthwhile to mention that it is in the Imphal East District that all the sampled entrepreneurs had attended such entrepreneurial development programmes. But majority of the Thoubal, Bishnupur, Senapati, Tamenglong Ukhrul and Chandel Districts' entrepreneurs did not consider it necessary to attend EDPs for their smooth running of their units.

After finding out whether the sampled entrepreneurs had attended EDPs or not, it will be very interesting to note the different agencies who had conducted these EDPs.

Table 2.12 shows that 9 out of 24 entrepreneurs who had attended EDPs mentioned SBI as the conducting agency as against 8 each who had attended EDPs conducted by AMEA and DIC.

2.12 Financing Pattern of Units

Finance is a highly versatile resource which demands proper utilization and planning. Financial discipline, information, forecasting, planning and control have a high profile in industrial management. In fact, the availability of enough finance is the

Table 2.12: Districts-wise EDP

Name of Districts		*EDP*		
		Yes	*No*	*Total*
Imphal East	Count	5	0	5
	% within Districts	100.0	.0	100.0
	% within EDP	19.2	.0	10.0
	% of Total	10.0	.0	10.0
Imphal West	Count	8	2	10
	% within Districts	80.0	20.0	100.0
	% within EDP	30.8	8.3	10.0
	% of Total	16.0	4.0	10.0
Thoubal	Count	1	4	5
	% within Districts	20.0	80.0	100.0
	% within EDP	3.8	16.7	10.0
	% of Total	2.0	8.0	10.0
Bishnupur	Count	2	3	5
	% within Districts	40.0	60.0	100.0
	% within EDP	7.7	12.5	10.0
	% of Total	4.0	6.0	10.0
Senapati	Count	1	4	5
	% within Districts	20.0	80.0	100.0
	% within EDP	3.8	16.7	10.0
	% of Total	2.0	8.0	10.0
Tamenglong	Count	2	3	5
	% within Districts	40.0	60.0	100.0
	% within EDP	7.7	12.5	10.0
	% of Total	4.0	6.0	10.0
Ukhrul	Count	2	3	5
	% within Districts	40.0	60.0	100.0
	% within EDP	7.7	12.5	10.0
	% of Total	4.0	6.0	10.0
Chandel	Count	2	3	5
	% within Districts	40.0	60.0	100.0
	% within EDP	7.7	12.5	10.0
	% of Total	4.0	6.0	10.0
Churachandpur	Count	3	2	5
	% within Districts	60.0	40.0	100.0
	% within EDP	11.5	8.3	10.0
	% of Total	6.0	4.0	10.0
Total	Count	26	24	50
	% within Districts	52.0	48.0	100.0
	% within EDP	100.0	100.0	100.0
	% of Total	52.0	48.0	100.0

Source: Field Survey.

Table 2.13: Agencies Conducting the EDPs

Name of District		EDP Conducting agencies					Total
		Not attended	AMEA	SBI	DIC	Others	
Imphal East	Count	0	0	2	2	1	5
	% within District	20	.0	40.0	40.0	20.0	100.0
	% within Agency	100	.0	22.2	25.0	100.0	10.0
	% of Total	200	.0	4.0	4.0	2.0	10.0
Imphal West	Count	2	5	1	2	0	10
	% within District	20.0	50.0	10.0	20.0	.0	100.0
	% within Agency	8.3	62.5	11.1	12.5	.0	20.0
	% of Total	4.0	10.0	2.0	4.0	.0	20.0
Thoubal	Count	4	0	0	1	0	5
	% within District	30.0	20.0	.0	20.0	.0	100.0
	% within Agency	16.7	12.5	.0	12.5	.0	10.0
	% of Total	8.0	2.0	.0	2.0	.0	10.0
Bishnupur	Count	3	1	1	0	0	5
	% within District	60.0	20.0	20.0	.0	.0	100.0
	% within Agency	12.5	12.5	11.1	.0	.0	10.0
	% of Total	6.0	6.0	2.0	.0	.0	10.0
Senapati	Count	4	0	1	0	0	5
	% within District	30.0	.0	20.0	20.0	.0	100.0
	% within Agency	16.7	.0	11.1	12.5	.0	10.0
	% of Total	8.0	.0	2.0	2.0	.0	10.0

(*Contd.*)

Table 2.13 (*Contd.*)

Tamenglong	Count	3	0	1	1	0	5
	% within District	60.0	.0	20.0	20.0	.0	100.0
	% within Agency	12.5	.0	11.1	12.5	.0	10.0
	% of Total	6.0	.0	2.0	2.0	.0	10.0
Ukhrul	Count	3	1	0	1	0	5
	% within District	60.0	20.0	.0	20.0	.0	100.0
	% within Agency	12.5	12.5	.0	12.5	.0	10.0
	% of Total	6.0	2.0	.0	2.0	.0	10.0
Chandel	Count	3	0	2	0	0	5
	% within District	60.0	.0	40.0	.0	.0	100.0
	% within Agency	12.5	.0	22.2	.0	.0	10.0
	% of Total	6.0	.0	4.0	.0	.0	10.0
Churachandpur	Count	2	1	1	1	0	5
	% within District	40.0	20.0	20.0	20.0	.0	100.0
	% within Agency	8.3	12.5	12.5	12.5	.0	10.0
	% of Total	4.0	2.0	2.0	2.0	.0	10.0
Total	Count	24	8	9	8	1	50
	% within District	48.0	16.0	18.0	16.0	2.0	100.0
	% within Agency	100.0	100.0	100.0	100.0	100.0	100.0
	% of Total	48.0	16.0	18.0	16.0	2.0	100.0

Source: Field Survey.

most important factor, without it, the idea to start business or industry will always remain a simple wish. Even if the necessary finance is available, there are many obstacles in financing the small scale industries. These obstacles are always rated as high risks. In fact, the risk element is present in every industrial financing. But more significantly, a special type of risk is associated with the small industry finance. This is because (a) small firms have a limited pool of management capabilities and business experience, (b) small firms are highly vulnerable to environment pressure, and (c) small firms are not always able to provide sufficient collateral to comply with assured repayment. Hence, financing a small scale industry is indeed a totally different problem in nature. Besides, the small units cannot enter the capital market on account of its organizational limitations. At the same time, the small entrepreneur is handicapped in his efforts to organize risk capital because his own savings are limited and his capacity to approach capital market is strictly limited. Therefore, he has to depend upon institutional and non-institutional sources for financing his unit.

Here, an attempt is made to assess the financial pattern of the sampled sick units as regards to its districts, form of organisation, generation and types of industries.

(i) District-wise Pattern of Financing

Table 2.14 tries to find out the district-wise pattern of financing, particularly relating to the average loan taken, outstanding and repaid by the sampled entrepreneurs. Regarding the average loan taken, the entrepreneurs hailing from Imphal West, Chandel, Imphal East and Ukhrul Districts have taken more loan than those from Thoubal, Senapati, Tamenglong, Bishnupur and Churachandpur Districts.

Quite interestingly, the hill districts of Ukhrul, Chandel and Churachandpur far exceed the other districts of the state as far as repayment of loans is concerned. While the average percentage of repayment of loans is 18.34, that of the above-mentioned hill districts are 28.92, 39.58 and 42.65 respectively. At the same time, among the valley districts, Bishnupur district

Table 2.14: District-wise Pattern of Financing

Districts	*Average loan taken(Rs.)*	*Average loan outstanding(Rs.)*	*Average loan repaid (Rs.)*	*% of repayment*
Imphal East	544411	1115000	41600	7.64
Imphal West	716200	1942500	25500	3.56
Thoubal	44000	58000	1000	2.27
Bishnupur	141000	178000	37000	26.24
Senapati	48000	73000	8000	16.67
Tamenglong	57000	63000	19000	33.33
Ukhrul	415000	800000	120000	28.92
Chandel	620000	755000	245400	39.58
Churachanpur	340000	680000	145000	42.65
Total	364181	760700	66800	18.34

Source: Field Survey.

fared well as regards to repayment of loans (26.24%) whereas that of Imphal East, Imphal West and Thoubal Districts is quite disheartening (less than 8%).

(ii) Form of Organisation-wise Pattern of Financing

As can be seen from Table 2.15, the average loan taken by partnership firms far more exceeds the overall average loan taken by the sampled units. Quite interestingly, on the other hand, the percentage of loan repayment is more for the partnership firms as compared to proprietorship form of organisation. While it is 41.29 per cent for the former, the latter's rate is only 13.63 per cent. It is quite obvious then, that proprietorship form of organisations are having more amount of loan outstanding, which at the same time, will go increasing with the passage of time.

(iii) Generation-wise Pattern of Financing

An attempt is made here to find out the generation of entrepreneurs' pattern of financing as regards to the sampled sick units. As already mentioned, the sampled units are run

Table 2.15: Form of Organisation-wise Pattern of Financing

Form of Organisation	*Average loan taken (Rs.)*	*Average loan outstanding (Rs.)*	*Average loan repaid (Rs.)*	*% of repayment*
Proprietorship	343387	781477	46818	13.63
Partnership	516666	608333	213333	41.29
Total	364181	760700	66800	18.34

Source: Field Survey.

by first and second generation entrepreneurs. As expected, the first generation entrepreneurs have taken more financial help than their other counterparts, which is even more than the overall average loan taken by the sampled units. But as regards to the habit of repayment of loan taken, these first generation entrepreneurs are still lagging behind the second generation entrepreneurs. It can be verified from Table 2.16 that only 17.88 per cent of the loan taken has been repaid back as against 24.51 per cent loan repayment rate made by the second generation entrepreneurs.

In other words, it can be concluded that the second generation entrepreneurs are more experienced as far as the repayment of loan is concerned.

(iv) Industry-wise Pattern of Financing

After finding the financing pattern of the sampled units as regards to various districts, forms of organisation and generation of entrepreneurs, it will be very interesting to know the industry-wise pattern of financing the sampled units. As can be seen from Table 2.17, the average loan taken by the plastic and rubber based industries is about the double of the overall average loan taken by the other sampled units. It is followed by food based and automobile and engineering units. But if compared with the rate of loan repayment, metal based and others' type of industries picture is far better than food based (only 13.24%), wood based (9.62%) and automobile and engineering units (9.28%). The rate of repayment of loan for the handlooms and handicrafts (23.40%) also exceeds the overall average rate of loan repayment.

Table 2.16: Generation-wise Pattern of Financing

Generation of Entrepreneur	*Average loan taken (Rs.)*	*Average loan outstanding (Rs.)*	*Average loan repaid (Rs.)*	*% of repayment*
First	434462	890128	77692	17.88
Second Generation	115000	301818	28181	24.51
Total	364181	760700	66800	18.34

Source: Field Survey.

Table 2.17: Industry-wise Pattern of Financing

Type of Industry	*Average loan taken (Rs.)*	*Average loan outstanding (Rs.)*	*Average loan repaid (Rs.)*	*% of repayment*
Food based	466538	1207692	61769	13.24
Metal based	386875	627500	129375	33.44
Handlooms and handicrafts	105000	165000	24571	23.40
Plastics and rubber based	898750	2100000	176250	19.61
Wood based	52000	72000	5000	9.62
Printing and stationery	208000	643750	38750	18.63
Automobile and engineering	454079	584285	42142	9.28
Others	224250	367500	75000	33.44
Total	364181	760700	66800	18.34

Source: Field Survey.

It can thus be concluded that the industry-wise rate of repayment of loan taken is quite discouraging as far as the sampled units are concerned.

References

1. Hirschamanian, A.H. (1958): "*The Strategy of Economic Development*", New York, p. 25.
2. Govt. of Manipur: "*Ninth Five Years'* Plan (1997-2002) and Annual Plan 1997-98."
3. Srivastava, S.S. and Yadav, R.A. "*Management and Monitoring of Industrial Sickness*", Concept Publishing Co., New Delhi, 1986, p. 195.

3

Causes of Sickness

3.1 Introduction

Sickness in industrial undertakings usually arises due to a complex of factors present in the internal and external environments. Internal environment pertains to the factors within the control of management whereas external environment relates to the factors beyond the control of the management.

Similar to these factors, for the present study, the causes of industrial sickness are broadly divided into the following heads:[1]

1. Internal Causes of Sickness

(a) Faulty project selection
(b) Marketing problems
(c) Financial problems
(d) Production problems
(e) Personnel problems
(f) Others

2. External Problems Relating to Banks and Other Financial Institutions

(a) Under-financing by banks

(b) Over-financing by banks
(c) Delay in disbursement of loans
(d) Delay in detection of early symptoms of sickness
(e) Delay in decision and action to rehabilitate the unit.
(f) Others.

3. Sickness made by Government

(a) Change in government policies
(b) Delayed in payment of bills by the government departments
(c) Red-tapism by government officials
(d) Others.

4. External Problems

(a) Raw-materials
(b) Power
(c) Marketing
(d) Labour
(e) Finance
(f) Others

5. Other External Problems

(a) Fire, flood, other natural calamities
(b) Other family problems
(c) Social problems like strikes, bandhs, insurgents, extortions, etc.

Taking into account the above-mentioned causes of industrial sickness, an attempt is being made here to analyze the findings of the study as follows:

3.2 District-wise Internal Causes of Sickness

Table 3.1 shows the district-wise internal causes of sickness. 40 per cent of the total sick units (20 units) had been caused by

Table 3.1: District-wise Internal Causes of Sickness

Name of Districts		*Internal Causes of sickness*				*Total*
		Faulty project selection	*Marketing problems*	*Finance problems*	*Production problems*	
Imphal East	Count	.0	2	3	.0	5
	% within District	.0	40.0	60.0	.0	100.0
	% within Causes	.0	20.0	15.0	.0	10.0
	% of Total	.0	4.0	6.0	.0	10.0
Imphal West	Count	2	1	4	3	10
	% within District	20.0	10.0	40.0	30.0	100.0
	% within Causes	16.7	10.0	20.0	37.5	20.0
	% of Total	4.0	2.0	2.0	6.0	20.0
Thoubal	Count	1	2	1	1	5
	% within District	20.0	40.0	20.0	20.0	100.0
	% within Causes	8.3	20.0	5.0	12.5	10.0
	% of Total	2.0	4.0	2.0	2.0	10.0
Bishnupur	Count	2	1	2	.0	5
	% within District	40.0	20.0	40.0	.0	100.0
	% within Causes	16.7	10.0	10.0	.0	10.0
	% of Total	4.0	2.0	4.0	.0	10.0

(Contd.)

Table 3.1 (*Contd.*)

Senapati	Count	1	.0	2	1	5
	% within District	20.0	.0	40.0	20.0	100.0
	% within Causes	8.3	.0	10.0	12.5	10.0
	% of Total	2.0	.0	4.0	2.0	10.0
Tamenglong	Count	3	1	.0	1	5
	% within District	60.0	20.0	.0	20.0	100.0
	% within Causes	25.0	10.0	.0	12.5	10.0
	% of Total	6.0	2.0	.0	2.0	10.0
Ukhrul	Count	2	2	.0	1	5
	% within District	40.0	40.0	.0	20.0	100.0
	% within Causes	16.7	20.0	.0	12.5	10.0
	% of Total	4.0	4.0	.0	2.0	10.0
Chandel	Count	.0	.0	3	2	5
	% within District	.0	.0	60.0	40.0	100.0
	% within Causes	.0	.0	15.0	25.0	10.0
	% of Total	.0	.0	6.0	4.0	10.0
Churachandpur	Count	1	1	3	.0	5
	% within District	20.0	20.0	60.0	.0	100.0
	% within Causes	8.3	10.0	15.0	.0	10.0
	% of Total	2.0	2.0	6.0	.0	10.0
Total	Count	12	10	20	8	50

internal financial problems. It is followed by faulty project selection (24%) and marketing problems (20%). Even among the districts studied, 80 per cent (4 units) of Senapati district suffered from financial problems, followed by 60 per cent each of the Imphal East, Chandel and Churachandpur districts. But, it is very surprising that sick units of Tamenglong and Ukhrul districts had no internal financial problems as compared to other districts. And as far as internal causes of sickness are concerned, it is found that there is no personnel problem in the units studied for industrial sickness.

Regarding production problems, units of Imphal West District suffered the most (37.5%), followed by Chandel district. At the same time, units of Imphal East, Thoubal and Ukhrul Districts are equally affected by marketing problems (20.0 % each).

3.3 District-wise External Problems Relating to Banks and other Financial Institutions

Availability of finances, that also in time, is very important for the smooth functioning of an enterprise. But, as can be seen from Table 3.2, 38 per cent (19 units) of the sampled sick units under study suffered from the severe problems of delay in disbursement of loans by banks and other financial institutions. Delay in detecting early symptoms of sickness (20.0%) and delay in decision and action to rehabilitate the unit (18.0%) also affected the units at their troublesome days of sickness. It is also an interesting scene where 8 per cent (4 units) of the sampled units had expressed an external problem due to over-financing by the banks.

As far as under-financing is concerned, Imphal East district suffered the most (37.5%) followed by Imphal West district.

3.4 District-wise Sickness made by Government

Sometimes, Government itself becomes the villain of these unfortunate sick industries. It can be proved from the Table 3.3 that 58 per cent of the total sampled units suffered from

Table 3.2: Districts-wise External Problems relating to Banks

Name of Districts		*External causes of sickness*					*Total*
		Under finan-cing by banks	*Over financing by banks*	*Delay in disbursement of loans*	*Delay in detecting early symptoms of sickness*	*Delay in decision and action to rehabilitate*	
Imphal East	Count	3	0	2	0	0	5
	% within District	60.0	.0	40.0	.0	.0	100.0
	% within Problems	37.5	.0	10.5	.0	.0	10.0
	% of Total	6.0	.0	4.0	.0	.0	10.0
Imphal West	Count	2	0	5	3	0	10
	% within District	20 0	.0	50.0	30.0	.0	100.0
	% within Problems	25.0	.0	26.3	30.0	.0	20.0
	% of Total	4.0	.0	10.0	6.0	.0	20.0
Thoubal	Count	0	0	1	3	1	5
	% within District	.0	.0	20.0	60.0	20.0	100.0
	% within Problems	.0	.0	5.3	30.0	11.1	10.0
	% of Total	.0	.0	2.0	6.0	2.0	10.0
Bishnupur	Count	0	2	3	0	0	5
	% within District	.0	40.0	60.0	.0	.0	100.0
	% within Problems	.0	50.0	15.8	.0	.0	10.0
	% of Total	.0	4.0	6.0	.0	.0	10.0
Senapati	Count	1	0	2	1	1	5
	% within District	20.0	.0	40.0	20.0	20.0	100.0
	% within Problems	12.5	.0	10.5	10.0	11.1	10.0
	% of Total	2.0	.0	4.0	2.0	2.0	10.0

(Contd)

Table 3.2 (*Contd.*)

Name of Districts		External causes of sickness					Total
		Under financing by banks	Over financing by banks	Delay in disbursement of loans	Delay in detecting early symptoms of sickness	Delay in decision and action to rehabilitate	
Tamenglong	Count	0	0	1	1	3	5
	% within District	.0	.0	20.0	20.0	60.0	100.0
	% within Problems	.0	.0	5.3	10.0	33.3	10.0
	% of Total	.0	.0	2.0	2.0	6.0	10.0
Ukhrul	Count	1	0	2	1	1	5
	% within District	20.0	.0	40.0	20.0	20.0	100.0
	% within Problems	12.5	.0	10.5	10.0	11.1	10.0
	% of Total	2.0	.0	4.0	2.0	2.0	10.0
Chandel	Count	0	1	2	1	1	5
	% within District	.0	20.0	40.0	20.0	20.0	100.0
	% within Problems	.0	25.0	10.5	10.0	11.1	10.0
	% of Total	.0	2.0	4.0	2.0	2.0	10.0
Chura-chandpur	Count	0	1	2	0	2	5
	% within District	.0	20.0	40.0	.0	40.0	100.0
	% within Problems	.0	25.0	10.5	.0	22.2	10.0
	% of Total	.0	2.0	4.0	.0	4.0	10.0
Total	Count	8	4	19	10	9	50
	% within District	16.0	8.0	38.0	20.0	18.0	100.0
	% within Problems	100.0	100.0	100.0	100.0	100.0	100.0
	% of Total	16.0	8.0	38.0	20.0	18.0	100.0

Source: Field Survey.

Table 3.3: District-wise Sickness made by Government

Name of Districts		Sickness made by government				Total
		Change in government policies	*Delay in payment of bills by govt. dept.*	*Red-tapism by govt. officers*	*Others*	
Imphal East	Count	2	1	2	0	5
	% within District	40.0	20.0	40.0	.0	100.0
	% within Sickness	15.4	25.0	6.9	.0	10.0
	% of Total	4.0	2.0	4.0	.0	10.0
Imphal West	Count	4	0.0	6	0	10
	% within District	40.0	0.0	60.0	.0	100.0
	% within Sickness	30.8	0.0	20.7	.0	20.0
	% of Total	8.0	0.0	12.0	.0	20.0
Thoubal	Count	1	2	2	0	5
	% within District	20.0	40.0	40.0	.0	100.0
	% within Sickness	7.7	50.0	6.9	.0	10.0
	% of Total	2.0	4.0	4.0	.0	10.0
Bishnupur	Count	1	0.0	3	1	5
	% within District	20.0	0.0	60.0	20.0	100.0
	% within Sickness	7.7	0.0	10 3	25.0	10.0
	% of Total	2.0	0.0	6.0	2.0	10.0
Senapati	Count	0	0.0	4	1	5
	% within District	.0	0.0	80.0	20.0	100.0
	% within Sickness	.0	0.0	13.8	25.0	10.0
	% of Total	.0	0.0	8.0	2.0	10.0

(Contd.)

Table 3.3 (*Contd.*)

Name of Districts		Sickness made by government				Total
		Change in government policies	Delay in payment of bills by govt. dept.	Red tapism by govt. officers	Others	
Tamenglong	Count	0.0	0.0	5	0.0	5
	% within District	0.0	0.0	100.0	0.0	100.0
	% within Sickness	0.0	0.0	17.2	0.0	10.0
	% of Total	0.0	0.0	10.0	0.0	10.0
Ukhrul	Count	0.0	1.0	4	.00	5
	% within District	0.0	20.0	80.0	0.0	100.0
	% within Sickness	0.0	25.0	13.8	0.0	10.0
	% of Total	0.0	2.0	8.0	0.0	10.0
Chandel	Count	3.0	0.0	0	2.0	5
	% within District	600.0	0.0	0.0	40.0	100.0
	% within Sickness	23.1	0.0	0.0	50.0	10.0
	% of Total	60.0	0.0	0.0	4.0	10.0
Churachandpur	Count	2.0	0.0	3	0.0	5
	% within District	400.0	0.0	60.0	0.0	100.0
	% within Sickness	15.4	0.0	10.3	0.0	10.0
	% of Total	40.0	0.0	6.0	0.0	10.0
Total	Count	13.0	4.0	29	0.4	50
	% within District	260.0	8.0	58.0	8.0	100.0
	% within Sickness	1000.0	100.0	100.0	100.0	100.0
	% of Total	260.0	8.0	58.0	8.0	100.0

Source: Field Survey.

red-tapism by government officers (29 units). No doubt, change in government policies was also a major factor (26.0%) as far as industrial sickness is concerned. In Senapati, Tamenglong and Ukhrul districts, red-tapism played the major role for industrial sickness. It was only an exception in Chandel District. Delay in payment of bills by Government departments was a major cause of sickness in Thoubal district as compared to other districts.

3.5 District-wise External Problems

Here, an attempt is made to ascertain the external problems being faced by the sick units.

Table 3.4 shows that maximum of the sampled units (38.0%) faced the problem of power as the external problem which are beyond their control. They had to availed power generators, thereby increasing the costs of products. 28 per cent of the units opined marketing as the major external problem as against finance problem (18.0%) and raw-materials (16.0%).

District-wise, power problems (40.0%) and marketing problems (30.0%) had caused as external problem responsible for industrial sickness in Imphal West District. But, finance problem played a major role (60.0%) in Senapati district for industrial sickness. It is worthwhile to mention that raw-materials are plenty in Churachandpur district for industrial development but marketing problem (60.0%) and power problem (40.0%) played major role for industrial sickness.

3.6 District-wise other External Problems

Social problems like strikes, bandhs, insurgents, extortions, etc. are acute external problems faced by the units. Economic blockades are so common on the two National Highways of Manipur. That's why it is not surprising to note that all the sample units, irrespective of its location, had expressed its uneasiness to cope up with all these external problems. Given the increasing insurgency problems in the state, outside entrepreneurs (innovative entrepreneurs) are hesitant to come

Table 3.4: District-wise External Problems

Name of Districts		*External Problems*				*Total*
		Raw materials	*Power*	*Marketing*	*Finance*	
Imphal East	Count	0	3	2	0	5
	% within District	.0	60.0	40.0	.0	100.0
	% within Problems	.0	15.8	14.3	.0	10.0
	% of Total	.0	6.0	4.0	.0	10.0
Imphal West	Count	1	4	3	2	10
	% within District	10.0	40.0	30.0	20.0	100.0
	% within Problems	12.5	21.1	21.4	22.2	20.0
	% of Total	2.0	8.0	6.0	4.0	20.0
Thoubal	Count	2	1	1	1	5
	% within District	40.0	20.0	20.0	20.0	100.0
	% within Problems	25.0	5.3	7.1	11.1	10.0
	% of Total	4.0	2.0	2.0	2.0	10.0
Bishnupur	Count	1	4	0	0	5
	% within District	20.0	80.0	.0	60.0	100.0
	% within Problems	12.5	21.1	.0	33.3	10.0
	% of Total	2.0	8.0	.0	6.0	10.0
Senapati	Count	0	1	1	3	5
	% within District	.0	20.0	20.0	60.0	100.0
	% within Problems	.0	5.3	7.1	33.3	10.0
	% of Total	.0	2.0	2.0	6.0	10.0
Tamenglong	Count	1	3	0	1	5
	% within District	20.0	60.0	.0	20.0	100.0
	% within Problems	12.5	5.3	.0	11.1	10.0
	% of Total	2.0	2.0	0	2.0	10.0
Ukhrul	Count	1	1	1	2	5
	% within District	20.0	20.0	20.0	40.0	100.0
	% within Problems	12.5	5.3	7.1	22.2	10.0
	% of Total	2.0	2.0	2.0	4.0	10.0
Chandel	Count	2	0	3	0	5
	% within District	40.0	.0	60.0	0	100.0
	% within Problems	25.0	.0	21.4	.0	10.0
	% of Total	4.0	.0	6.0	.0	10.0
Churachandpur	Count	0	2	3	0	5
	% within District	.0	40.0	60.0	.0	100.0
	% within Problems	.0	10.5	21.4	.0	10.0
	% of Total	.0	4.0	6.0	.0	10.0
Total	Count	8	19	14	9	50
	% within District	16.0	38.0	28.0	18.0	100.0
	% within Problems	100.0	100.0	100.0	100.0	100.0
	% of Total	16.0	38.0	28.0	18.0	100.0

Source: Field Survey.

to the insurgency stricken state for establishing their industrial units.[2] These external problems (Table 3.5) have its long lasting implications for the industrial and overall development of the state.

3.7 District-wise Rehabilitation Package

It is very surprising to note that till date, the state Government or any financial institute has not yet declared a unit as sick unit in Manipur. So, there is no question of rehabilitation package in the state. Some of the sampled units have tried to convince the concerned banks, Industries Deptt. And even the state Government to declare their units as sick units under the umbrella of All Manipur Entrepreneurs Assn. (AMEA).[3] Till date, the concerned authorities are not taking up the required formalities of declaration of sick units and hence, no package of rehabilitation for these units (Table 3.6)

3.8 Organisation-wise Internal Causes of Sickness

Table 3.7 tried to analyse the organization-wise internal causes of sickness. As can be seen, financial problems played a major role (43.2%) for industrial sickness in units which are organised as sole proprietorship, followed by faulty project selection (22.7%) and marketing problems (20.5%). In the case of partnership firms under study, faulty project selection and production problems (33.3 % each) were equally responsible for industrial sickness as internal causes.

3.9 Organisation-wise External Problems Relating to Banks and other Financial Institutions

It will be very interesting to study the external problems related with banks and other financial institutions from the point of view of different types of organizations. Proprietorship form of industrial units had suffered maximum from delay in disbursement of loans (38.6%), followed by under-financing and delay in decision and action to rehabilitate the units (18.2 % each). But, it is very noteworthy that partnership firms

Table 3.5: District-wise other External Problems

Name of Districts		Other external Problems: Social problems like strike, bandhs, insurgents, extortions	Total
Imphal East	Count	5	5
	% within District	100.0	100.0
	% within Problems	10.0	10.0
	% of Total	10.0	10.0
Imphal West	Count	10	10
	% within District	100.0	100.0
	% within Problems	20.0	20.0
	% of Total	20.0	20.0
Thoubal	Count	5	5
	% within District	100.0	100.0
	% within Problems	10.0	10.0
	% of Total	10.0	10.0
Bishnupur	Count	5	5
	% within District	100.0	100.0
	% within Problems	10.0	10.0
	% of Total	10.0	10.0
Senapati	Count	5	5
	% within District	100.0	100.0
	% within Problems	10.0	10.0
	% of Total	10.0	10.0
Tamenglong	Count	5	5
	% within District	100.0	100.0
	% within Problems	10.0	10.0
	% of Total	10.0	10.0
Ukhrul	Count	5	5
	% within District	100.0	100.0
	% within Problems	10.0	10.0
	% of Total	10.0	10.0
Chandel	Count	5	5
	% within District	100.0	100.0
	% within Problems	10.0	10.0
	% of Total	10.0	10.0
Churachandpur	Count	5	5
	% within District	100.0	100.0
	% within Problems	10.0	10.0
	% of Total	10.0	10.0
Total	Count	50	50
	% within District	100.0%	100.0%
	% within Problems	100.0%	100.0%
	% of Total	100.0%	100.0%

Source: Field Survey.

Table 3.6: Districts-wise Rehabilitation of Sick Units

Name of Districts		*Any rehabilitation*	*Total*
		No	
Imphal East	Count	5	5
	% within District	100.0	100.0
	% within Rehabilitation	10.0	10.0
	% of Total	10.0	10.0
Imphal West	Count	10	10
	% within District	100.0	100.0
	% within Rehabilitation	20.0	20.0
	% of Total	20.0	20.0
Thoubal	Count	5	5
	% within District	100.0	100.0
	% within Rehabilitation	10.0	10.0
	% of Total	10.0	10.0
Bishnupur	Count	5	5
	% within District	100.0	100.0
	% within Rehabilitation	10.0	10.0
	% of Total	10.0	10.0
Senapati	Count	5	5
	% within District	100.0	100.0
	% within Rehabilitation	10.0	10.0
	% of Total	10.0	10.0
Tamenglong	Count	5	5
	% within District	100.0	100.0
	% within Rehabilitation	10.0	10.0
	% of Total	10.0	10.0
Ukhrul	Count	5	5
	% within District	100.0	100.0
	% within Rehabilitation	10.0	10.0
	% of Total	10.0	10.0
Chandel	Count	5	5
	% within District	100.0	100.0
	% within Rehabilitation	10.0	10.0
	% of Total	10.0	10.0
Churachandpur	Count	5	5
	% within District	100.0	100.0
	% within Rehabilitation	10.0	10.0
	% of Total	10.0	10.0
Total	Count	50	50
	% within District	100.0%	100.0%
	% within Rehabilitation	100.0%	100.0%
	% of Total	100.0%	100.0%

Source: Field Survey.

Table 3.7: Organisation-wise Internal Causes of Sickness

Form of Organisation		*Internal causes of sickness*				*Total*
		Faulty project selection	*Marketing problems*	*Finance problems*	*Production problems*	
Prcprietorship	Count	10	9	19	6	44
	% within Organisation	22.7	20.5	43.2	13.6	100.0
	% within Internal causes	83.3	90.0	95.0	75.0	88.0
	% of Total	20.0	18.0	38.0	12.0	88.0
Partnership	Count	2	1	1	2	6
	% within Organisation	33.3	16.7	16.7	33.3	100.0
	% within Internal causes	16.7	10.0	5.0	25.0	12.0
	% of Total	4.0	2.0	2.0	4.0	12.0
Total	Count	12	10	20	8	50
	% within Organisation	24.0	20.0	40.0	16.0	100.0
	% within Internal causes	100.0	100.0	100.0	100.0	100.0
	% of Total	24.0	20.0	40.0	16.0	100.0

Source: Field Survey.

had no problem with under-financing and over-financing by banks (Table 3.8). It was delay in detecting early symptoms of sickness (50.0%) that resulted into sickness for the partnership firms, followed by delay in disbursement of loans (33.3%).

3.10 Organisation-wise Sickness made by Government

Red-tapism by government officers is also an important cause of sickness being faced by the sampled units irrespective of their forms of organization. Table 3.9 analyses this factor and found that 56.8 per cent of proprietorship and 66.7 per cent of partnership firms faced this problem and referred to it as the major cause of sickness made by government. Other than this, change in Government policies also affected 27.3 per cent (12 units) of the proprietorship units in the process of becoming sick units.

3.11 Organisation-wise External Problems

As shown by Table 3.10, power problems resulted into industrial sickness for maximum of the units under study. 36.4 per cent of proprietorship units and 50 per cent of partnership firms had suffered the problems of power scarcity as external problem. Next to power, marketing problems of proprietorship units are also acute as it affected 31.8 per cent of the said units. Financial problems had also played an adverse role for the partnership firms. But, it is interesting to note that partnership firms had no problem as regards to marketing of its products.

3.12 Industry-wise Internal Causes of Sickness

Contrary to plastics and rubber, printing and stationery and automobile and engineering industries, food based industries, faced marketing problems (46.2%) as the main internal cause of sickness. As can be seen from Table 3.11, financial problems also caused serious problems for food based industries (30.8%). On the other hand, faulty project selection and financial problems affected adversely on automobile and engineering

Table 3.8: Organisation-wise External Causes of Sickness

Form of Organisation		*External causes of sickness*					*Total*
		Under-financing by banks	*Over-financing by banks*	*Delay in disbursement of loans*	*Delay in defecting early symptoms of sickness*	*Delay in decision and action to rehabilitate the unit*	
Proprietorship	Count	8	4	17	7	8	44
	% within Organisation	18.2	9.1	38.6	15.9	18.2	100.0
	% within Causes	100.0	100.0	89.5	70.0	88.9	88.0
	% of Total	16.0	8.0	34.0	14.0	16.0	88.0
Partnership	Count	.0	.0	2	3	1	6
	% within Organisation	.0	.0	33.3	50.0	16.7	100.0
	% within Causes	.0	.0	10.5	30.0	11.1	12.0
	% of Total	.0	.0	4.0	6.0	2.0	12.0
Total	Count	8	4	19	10	9	50
	% within Organisation	16.0	8.0	38.0	20.0	18.0	100.0
	% within Causes	100.0	100.0	100.0	100.0	100.0	100.0
	% of Total	16.0	8.0	38.0	20.0	18.0	100.0

Source: Field Survey.

Table 3.9: Ownership-wise Sickness made by Governments

Form of organisation		*Sickness made by Governments*				*Total*
		Change in Govt. policies	*Delay in payment of bills by Govt. Deptt.*	*Red-tapism by Govt. officers*	*Others*	
Proprietorship	Count	12	3	25	4.0	44.0
	% within Organisation	27.3	6.8	56.8	9.1	100.0
	% within Sickness	92.3	75.0	86.2	100.0	88.0
	% of Total	24.0	6.0	50.0	8.0	88.0
Partnership	Count	1	1	4	0.0	6.0
	% within Organisation	16.7	16.7	66.7	0.0	100.0
	% within Sickness	7.7	25.0	13.8	0.0	12.0
	% of Total	2.0	2.0	8.0	0.0	12.0
Total	Count	13	4	29	4.0	50.0
	% within Organisation	26.0	8.0	58.0	8.0	100.0
	% within Sickness	100.0	100.0	100.0	100.0	100.0
	% of Total	26.0	8.0	58.0	8.0	100.0

Source: Field Survey.

Table 3.10: Organisation-wise External Problems

Form of organisation		*External Problems*				*Total*
		Raw Materials	*Power*	*Marketing*	*Finance*	
Proprietorship	Count	7	16	14	7	44
	% within Organisation	15.9	36.4	31.8	15.9	100.0
	% within Problems	87.5	84.2	100.0	77.8	88.0
	% of Total	14.0	32.0	28.0	14.0	88.0
Partnership	Count	1	3	0	2	6
	% within Organisation	16.7	50.0	.0	33.3	100.0
	% within Problems	12.5	15.8	.0	22.2	12.0
	% of Total	2.0	6.0	.0	4.0	12.0
Total	Count	8	19	14	9	50
	% within Organisation	16.0	38.0	28.0	18.0	100.0
	% within Problems	100.0	100.0	100.0	100.0	100.0
	% of Total	16.0	38.0	28.0	18.0	100.0

Source: Field Survey.

Table 3.11: Industry-wise Internal Causes of Sickness

Type of Industry		*Internal causes of sickness*				*Total*
		Faulty project selection	*Marketing problems*	*Finance problems*	*Production problems*	
Food based	Count	2	6	4	1	13
	% within Industry	15.4	46.2	30.8	7.7	100.0
	% within Causes	16.7	60.0	20.0	12.5	26.0
	% of Total	4.0	12.0	8.0	2.0	26.0
Metal based	Count	2	2	1	3	8
	% within Industry	25.0	25.0	12.5	37.5	100.0
	% within Causes	16.7	20.0	5.0	37.5	16.0
	% of Total	4.0	4.0	2.0	6.0	16.0
Handlooms and handicrafts	Count	2	1	3	1	7
	% within Industry	28.6	14.3	42.9	14.3	100.0
	% within Causes	16.7	10.0	15.0	12.5	14.0
	% of Total	4.0	2.0	6.0	2.0	14.0
Plastics and rubber based	Count	1	0	2	1	4
	% within Industry	25.0	.0	50.0	25.0	100.0
	% within Causes	8.3	.0	10.0	12.5	8.0
	% of Total	2.0	.0	4.0	2.0	8.0
Wood based	Count	1	1	3	0	5
	% within Industry	20.0	20.0	60.0	.0	100.0
	% within Causes	8.3	10.0	15.0	.0	10.0
	% of Total	2.0	2.0	6.0	.0	10.0

(Contd.)

Table 3.11 (*Contd.*)

Type of Industry		*Internal causes of sickness*				*Total*
		Faulty project selection	*Marketing problems*	*Finance problems*	*Production problems*	
Printing and stationery	Count	1.0	0.0	3.0	0.0	4.0
	% within Industry	25.0	.0	75.0	0.0	100.0
	% within Causes	8.3	.0	15.0	0.0	8.0
	% of Total	2.0	.0	6.0	0.0	8.0
Automobile and Engineering	Count	3.0	0.0	3.0	1.0	7.0
	% within Industry	42.9	.0	42.9	14.3	100.0
	% within Causes	25.0	.0	15.0	12.5	14.0
	% of Total	6.0	.0	6.0	2.0	14.0
Others	Count	0.0	0.0	1.0	1.0	2.0
	% within Industry	0.0	.0	50.0	50.0	100.0
	% within Causes	0.0	.0	5.0	12.5	4.0
	% of Total	0.0	.0	2.0	2.0	4.0
Total	Count	12.0	10.0	20.0	8.0	50.0
	% within Industry	24.0	20.0	40.0	16.0	100.0
	% within Causes	100.0	100.0	100.0	100.0	100.0
	% of Total	24.0	20.0	40.0	16.0	100.0

Source: Field Survey.

industries (42.9 per cent each). Maximum of the handlooms and handicrafts industries (42.9%) also suffered from financial problems. But, it is interesting to note that production problems had been a major internal problem to metal based industries (37.5%) than to other types of industries.

3.13 Industry-wise External Problems Relating to Banks and other Financial Institutions

Table 3.12 tried to analyse the external problems relating to the banks and other financial institutions from the point of view of different types of industries. As can be seen, maximum of the food based industries suffered from delay in disbursement of loans (38.5%). On the other hand, it was under-financing by banks that had adversely affected plastics and rubber based industries (75.0%). In the case of automobile and engineering industries, the main problem was delay in disbursement of loans (57.1%) and delay in decision and action to rehabilitate the unit (28.6%). It is also noteworthy that maximum of the units found to be over financed by banks are food based (50.0%), handlooms and handicrafts (25.0%) and automobile and engineering units (25.0%).

3.14 Industry-wise Sickness made by Government

Majority of the food based industries highlighted red-tapism by government officers as the major cause of sickness made by Government (69.2%). Table 3.13 has shown the same trend for other types of industries also. Not surprisingly, red-tapism alone was the only cause of sickness made by Government for wood based industries.

On the other hand, change in Government policies had also affected adversely to food based and handlooms and handicrafts industries (23.1 % each). But for the plastics and rubber based industries, it was delay in payment of bills by Government departments that became a major cause of industrial sickness made by Government (50.0%)

Table 3.12: Industry-wise External Causes of Sickness

Type of Industry		*External causes of sickness*					*Total*
		Under-financing by banks	*Over-financing by banks*	*Delay in disbursement of loans*	*Delay in defecting early symptoms of sickness*	*Delay in decision and action to rehabilitate the unit*	
Food based	Count	2.0	2 0	5.0	2.0	2.0	13.0
	% within Industry	15.4	15 4	38.5	15.4	15.4	100.0
	% within Causes	25.0	50.0	26.3	20.0	22.2	26.0
	% of Total	4.0	4.0	10.0	4.0	4.0	26.0
Metal based	Count	0.0	0.0	4.0	3.0	1	8.0
	% within Industry	0.0	0.0	50.0	37.5	12.5	100.0
	% within Causes	0.0	0.0	21.11	30.0	11.1	16.0
	% of Total	0.0	0.0	8.0	6.0	2.0	16.0
Handlooms and handicrafts	Count	2.0	1.0	1.0	1.0	2	7.0
	% within Industry	28.6	14.3	14.3	14.3	28.6	100.0
	% within Causes	25.0	25.0	5.3	10.0	22.2	14.0
	% of Total	4.0	2.0	2.0	2.0	4.0	14.0
Plastics and rubber based	Count	3.0	0.0	0.0	1.0	0	4.0
	% within Industry	75.0	0.0	0.0	25.0	.0	100.0
	% within Causes	37.5	0.0	0.0	10.0	.0	8.0
	% of Total	6.0	0.0	0.0	2.0	.0	8.0
Wood based	Count	0.0	0.0	2.0	2.0	1	5.0
	% within Industry	0.0	0.0	40.0	40.0	25.0	100.0
	% within Causes	0.0	0.0	10.5	20.0	11.1	10.0
	% of Total	0.0	0.0	4.0	4.0	2.0	10.0

(Contd.)

Table 3.12 (*Contd.*)

Type of Industry		*External causes of sickness*					*Total*
		Under financing by banks	*Over financing by banks*	*Delay in disbursement of loans*	*Delay in defecting early symptoms of sickness*	*Delay in decision and action to rehabilitate the unit*	
Printing and stationery	Count	1.0	0.0	1.0	1.0	1.0	4.0
	% within Industry	25.0	0.0	25.0	25.0	25.0	100.0
	% within Causes	12.5	0.0	5.3	10.0	11.1	8.0
	% of Total	2.0	0.0	2.0	2.0	2.0	8.0
Automobile and Engineering	Count	0.0	1.0	4.0	0.0	2.0	7.0
	% within Industry	0.0	14.3	57.1	0.0	28.6	100.0
	% within Causes	0.0	25.0	21.1	0.0	22.2	14.0
	% of Total	0.0	2.0	8.0	0.0	4.0	14.0
Others	Count	0.0	0.0	2.0	0.0	0.0	2.0
	% within Industry	0.0	0.0	100.0	0.0	0.0	100.0
	% within Causes	0.0	0.0	10.5	0.0	0.0	4.0
	% of Total	0.0	0.0	4.0	0.0	0.0	4.0
Total	Count	8.0	4.0	19.0	10.0	9.0	50.0
	% within Industry	16.0	8.0	38.0	20.0	18.0	100.0
	% within Causes	100.0	100.0	100.0	100.0	100.0	100.0
	% of Total	16.0	8.0	38.0	20.0	18.0	100.0

Source: Field Survey.

Table 3.13: Industry-wise Sickness made by Governments

Type of industry		*Sickness made by governments*				
		Change in Government policies	*Delay in payment of bills by Govt. deptt.*	*Red-tapism by Govt. officers.*	*Others*	*Total*
Food based	Count	0.5	0.0	0.5	0.1	13.0
	% within industry	23.1	0.0	69.2	7.7	100.0
	% within Sickness	23.1	0.0	31.0	25.0	26.0
	% of Total	6.0	0.0	18.0	2.0	26.0
Metal based	Count	0.2	0.1	0.4	1.0	0.8
	% within industry	25.0	12.5	50.0	12.5	100.0
	% within Sickness	15.4	25.0	13.8	25.0	16.0
	% of Total	4.0	2.0	8.0	2.0	16.0
Handlooms and handicrafts	Count	0.3	0.1	0.3	0.0	0.7
	% within industry	42.9	14.3	42.9	0.0	100.0
	% within Sickness	23.1	25.0	10.3	0.0	14.0
	% of Total	6.0	2.0	6.0	0.0	14.0
Plastics and rubber based	Count	0.1	0.2	0.1	0.0	0.4
	% within industry	25.0	50.0	25.0	0.0	100.0
	% within Sickness	7.7	50.0	3.4	0.0	8.0
	% of Total	2.0	4.0	2.0	0.0	8.0
Wood based	Count	0.0	0.0	0.5	0.0	0.5
	% within industry	0.0	0.0	100.0	0.0	100.0
	% within Sickness	0.0	0.0	17.2	0.0	10.0
	% of Total	0.0	0.0	10.0	0.0	10.0

(Contd.)

Table 3.13 (*Contd.*)

Type of industry		Sickness made by governments				
		Change in Government policies	Delay in payment of bills by Govt. dept.	Red tapism by Govt. officers.	Others	Total
Printing and stationery	Count	1.0	0.0	0.2	1.0	4.0
	% within industry	25.0	0.0	50.0	25.0	100.0
	% within Sickness	7.7	0.0	6.9	25.0	8.0
	% of Total	2.0	0.0	4.0	2.0	8.0
Automobile and Engineering	Count	2.0	0.0	0.4	1.0	7.0
	% within industry	28.6	0.0	57.1	14.3	100.0
	% within Sickness	15.4	0.0	13.8	25.0	14.0
	% of Total	4.0	0.0	8.0	2.0	14.0
Others	Count	1.0	0.0	0.1	0.0	2.0
	% within industry	50.0	0.0	50.0	0.0	100.0
	% within Sickness	7.7	0.0	3.4	0.0	14.0
	% of Total	2.0	0.0	2.0	0.0	14.0
Total	Count	13.0	4.0	29.0	0.4	50.0
	% within industry	26.0	8.0	58.0	8.0	100.0
	% within Sickness	100.0	100.0	100.0	100.0	100.0
	% of Total	26.0	8.0	58.0	8.0	100.0

Source: Field Survey.

3.15 Industry-wise External Problems

It is a well-known fact that Manipur is a power starved state. All the industrial units had suffered this problem since a long-time. But, as can be seen from Table 3.14, food based industries suffered the most (26.3%), followed by metal based (21.1%) and automobile and engineering (15.8%) industries. Again, raw-materials problems scenes to be acute for food based industries (50.0%), followed by metal based industries (25.0%).

Industry-wise, marketing problems of handlooms and handicrafts industries was noteworthy while it has no raw-material problem. All the different types of industries had financial problems more or less the same, only with the exception of plastics and rubber based and printing and stationery industries.

3.16 Conclusion

Over and above the foregoing causes, it was found from the field survey that most of the sampled units lack financial discipline and information and hardly have they resorted to financial planning and forecasting with no long term prospective in mind. One hardly comes across among the units preparing cash flow statement. If any authority even wanted to rehabilitate these sick units, the financial statements of the units have to be analysed. But in its absence, the process itself is big problem.

Another serious problem being faced by majority of the sampled units is that of competition from large scale industries, out of state and even from foreign countries. In the case of Manipur, recent development has shown that trade has become inextricably linked with the development process. Any prolonged disruption in trade can destabilize the standard of living of the people significantly. The pattern of development in the state has been such that it has come to depend extensively on imports from other states even for the minimal day-to-day requirements. A large, volume of goods including the daily necessities is imported into the state from different parts of the country as well as from Myanmar via Moreh. There is no significant item of export from Manipur.[4]

Table 3.14: Industry-wise External Problems

Type of Industry		External Problems				
		Raw materials	*Power*	*Marketing*	*Finance*	*Total*
Food based	Count	4.0	5.0	3.0	1.0	13.0
	% within Industry	30.8	38.5	23.1	7.7	100.0
	% within Problems	50.0	26.3	21.4	11.1	26.0
	% of Total	8.0	10.0	6.0	2.0	26.0
Metal based	Count	2.0	4.0	0.0	2.0	8.0
	% within Industry	25.0	50.0	0.0	25.0	100.0
	% within Problems	25.0	21.1	0.0	22.2	16.0
	% of Total	4.0	8.0	0.0	4.0	16.0
Handlooms and handicrafts	Count	0.0	2.0	3.0	2.0	7.0
	% within Industry	0.0	28.6	42.9	28.6	100.0
	% within Problems	0.0	10.5	21.4	22.2	14.0
	% of Total	0.0	4.0	6.0	4.0	14.0
Plastics and rubber based	Count	0.0	2.0	2.0	0.0	4.0
	% within Industry	0.0	50.0	50.0	0.0	100.0
	% within Problems	0.0	10.5	14.3	0.0	8.0
	% of Total	0.0	4.0	4.0	0.0	8.0
Wood based	Count	1.0	1.0	1.0	2.0	5.0
	% within Industry	20.0	20.0	20.0	40.0	100.0
	% within Problems	12.5	5.3	7.1	22.2	10.0
	% of Total	2.0	2.0	2.0	4.0	10.0

(*Contd.*)

Table 3.14 (*Contd.*)

Type of Industry		*External Problems*				
		Raw materials	*Power*	*Marketing*	*Finance*	*Total*
Printing and stationery	Count	1.0	1.0	2.0	0.0	4.0
	% within Industry	25.0	25.0	50.0	0.0	100.0
	% within Problems	12.5	5.3	14.3	0.0	8.0
	% of Total	2.0	2.0	4.0	0.0	8.0
Automobile and Engineering	Count	0.0	3.0	3.0	1.0	7.0
	% within Industry	0.0	42.9	42.9	14.3	100.0
	% within Problems	0.0	15.8	21.4	11.1	14.0
	% of Total	0.0	6.0	6.0	2.0	14.0
Others	Count	0.0	1.0	0.0	1.0	2.0
	% within Industry	0.0	50.0	0.0	50.0	100.0
	% within Problems	0.0	5.3	0.0	11.1	4.0
	% of Total	0.0	2.0	0.0	2.0	4.0
Total	Count	8.0	19.0	14.0	9.0	50.0
	% within Industry	16.0	38.0	28.0	18.0	100.0
	% within Problems	100.0	100.0	100.0	100.0	100.0
	% of Total	16.0	38.0	28.0	18.0	100.0

Source: Field Survey.

Export of handloom and handicraft product also has decreased substantially in recent years. The competition from big mills in the mainland both in price and marketing has crippled a thriving export sector. The free-trade policy of Britain in the nineteenth century and the competition from mainland products have posed a serious threat to the process of industrialization in this state. This threat has been compounded with the opening of the Indo-Myanmar border trade. Goods of daily use are now imported from Myanmar at significantly lower prices. This practically smothered any nascent impulse for industrialization. The local producers can no longer supply goods at prices as low as those imported items. This led to the gradual death of many small-scale industrial units. The economy thus became a captive market for the industrial products of the mainland as well as the imports from Myanmar. The emerging pattern of trade has simply strengthened the economic power enjoyed by the outsiders to control the state's economy. The problem of this power is that people from outside the state in general have not been making any significant investment for the development of the economic infrastructure of the state. They were interested in extracting the maximum profit out of their transaction. It is a well-known fact that in the course of their business transactions, traders have to pay protection money to a large number of unlawful organizations operating in and outside Manipur. This type of payment invariably raises their transaction cost and this leads to a reduction in their profit margin. However, big merchants involved in wholesale trade have successfully managed to transfer this burden to the consumers. As a result, in spite of substantial transport subsidies and tax concessions enjoyed by industrialists in this region the price of commodities has generally been on the higher side *vis-à-vis* the mainland.

The point is how to make trade an engine of growth sustainable in every sense. The high vulnerability of the economy and the standard of living to external shocks including disruption in the National Highways is not a positive aspect of growth. Ideally speaking, every section of the society should have a share in the benefits of growth generated by any means including trade. Such a process can be realized only when we have an adequate knowledge of resource potential of the state. It is a fact that the IT revolution has significantly influenced the pattern of demand. A strategy is needed to ensure that our resource-base is utilized with due consideration for comparative advantage in line with the emerging pattern of demand. If our consumption needs cannot be produced competitively in Manipur, we should ensure that we have the means to procure our needs both physically and financially.

References

1. Mathur, Satish B. *op. cit.*
2. Singh, Kh. Tomba, *op. cit.*
3. President AMEA.
4. Singh, Priyokumar, Th. "*Dynamics of Trade in Manipur (1950-2006)*" Unpublished Ph.D. Thesis submitted to Manipur University in 2002.

4
Remedies of Industrial Sickness in Manipur

4.1 Introduction

During the past few years, sickness in industries has become a very thought provoking and obvious offshoot of the modern jet age industrial society. It is, however, not a very recent phenomenon and certainly not peculiar only to India. It has become all pervading, touching all countries. But its recent growth and magnitude, recently, is so rapid that it has assumed unmanageable proportions in India in general and in Manipur in particular. It is a continuous process and painful reality of rapid industrialization which starts right from the very beginning of industrialization. The question, now, is how to safeguard properly and utilize effectively the sunken capital of the public and the private institutions in sick units. It is nothing but a choice between opportunity cost for nursing sick units and closure of a large number of sick units thereby resulting into social lost of the economy and a dampening effect on the new ventures in Manipur.

A number of remedies are in practice for retrieving of industrial sickness in India. Institutions like the Government, IRCI, RBI, IDBI, IFCI, ICICI, banks, etc.[1] have its own package programme for creation of sickness. It is thus, proposed in this chapter that the role played by various institutions and their popular schemes of retrieving sickness will be of much use to all the concerned entrepreneurs in particular and society in general for prevention of industrial sickness.

Major reasons for industrial sickness in Manipur can be prevented if we ensure:

(i) that the project is viable.
(ii) that the approved and clearance for finance and the assistance are available in time under simplified procedures and one windows service.
(iii) that there is no delay in clearance for importing capital goods and raw materials.
(iv) that the project is implemented and commenced as per schedule.
(v) that the action to modify the product mix is in time if there are changes in the market demand.
(vi) that there is uninterrupted power supply for the industrial purpose.
(vii) that the entrepreneurs are sincere, efficient and accountable and at the same time, punishment must be awarded for delay, negligence, mismanagement of mis-utilisation of funds.
(viii) that only the required number of manpower is recruited based on efficiency, skill and competency.
(ix) that there is healthy and cordial labour relations.
(x) last, but not the least, there is effective systems and controls at all levels of operations.

The following assistances and incentives will be very helpful in preventing the industrial sickness in Manipur keeping into consideration the above facts and figures, the following strategies has to be adopted for prevention of industrial sickness:

(a) no loan on the specific project till the project becomes economically viable
(b) full exemption from custom duty on all capital imports
(c) holiday on tax
(d) transport subsidy

(e) incentives for increased output
(f) rewards and recognition for full capacity utilization
(g) assistance in marketing of products

4.2 Role of Banks and Other Financial Institutions

The steps to be taken to rehabilitate sick units are far more important than the establishment of units. In this context, banks and other institutions must play a significant role. In fact, the funds already invested in sick units can be realized if these units are revived. If they are not rehabilitated, then they may sink and have to be closed down.

Small Scale Industries (SSI) constitutes an important and crucial segment of the industrial sector. This has been acknowledged by the Government of India by the high priority it has accorded to the SSI sector. The Reserve Bank of India has also bestowed the status of Priority Sector to SSI lending by banks and various circulars/guidelines have been issued in this regard from time to time. Several internal and external factors have put considerable pressure on the performance of the SSIs, resulting in a number of them becoming sick. Of late, the incidence of sickness in SSI Sector is showing an increasing trend and a large number of SSI units, identified as sick, and was not found potentially viable.

To address this, and other allied issues, the Group of Ministers on SSI, in their meeting held on 16th August, 2000, had desired that RBI should draw up a revised, detailed, transparent and non-discretionary guidelines for rehabilitation of current sick and potentially viable SSI units. Accordingly, a Working Group on Rehabilitation of Sick SSI was constituted by RBI in November 2000 with the Chairman, Indian Banks' Association, Shri S.S. Kohli, as its Chairman. The Group has since submitted its report and all the major recommendations made therein, including a change in the criteria for identification and classification of sick units in the SSI Sector, have been accepted by the Reserve Bank of India. The draft revised guidelines were put on RBI website and also circulated among banks, SSI Association, etc. for eliciting their views. The suggestions received have been considered while finalizing the revised guidelines drawn up on the basis of the recommendations of the Working Group.

The revised guidelines are issued for rehabilitation of sick units in the SSI sector as given below:

I. General Guidelines for Rehabilitation of Sick SSI Units

(a) Incipient Sickness

(i) It is of utmost importance to take measures to ensure that sickness is arrested at the incipient stage itself. The branch officials should keep a close watch on the operations in the account and take adequate measures to achieve this objective. The managements of the units financed by banks should be advised about their primary responsibility to inform the banks if they face problems which could lead to sickness and to restore the units to normal health. The organizational arrangements at branch level should also be fully geared for early detection of sickness and prompt remedial action. Banks/Financial Institutions will have to identify the units showing symptoms of sickness by effective monitoring and provide additional finance, if warranted, so as to bring back the units to a healthy track. An illustrative list of warning signals of incipient sickness that are thrown up during the scrutiny of borrowal accounts and other related records e.g. periodical financial data, stock statements, reports on inspection of factory premises and godowns, etc. Further, the system of asset classification introduced in banks will be useful for detecting advances, which are deteriorating in quality well in time. The bank should make full enquiry into the financial health of the unit, its operations, etc. and take remedial action. The branch officials who are familiar with the day-to-day operations in the borrowal accounts should be under obligation to identify the early warning signals and initiate corrective steps promptly. Such steps may include providing timely financial assistance depending on established need, if it is within the powers of the branch manager, and an early reference to the controlling office where the relief required are beyond his delegated powers. The branch manager may also help the unit, in sorting out difficulties which are non-financial in nature and require assistance from outside agencies like Government departments/undertakings, Electricity Boards, etc. He should also keep the term lending institutions informed about the position of the units wherever they are also involved.

(ii) The instructions issued to banks by RBI to set up cells at all regional centres, besides at Head Office, to deal with sick industrial units and also provide expert staff including technical personnel to such cells are reiterated.

(b) Viability of Sick SSI Units

A unit may be regarded as potentially viable if it would be in a position, after implementing a relief package spread over a period not exceeding five years from the commencement of the package from banks, financial institutions, Government (Central/State) and other concerned agencies, as may be necessary, to continue to service its repayment obligations as agreed upon including those forming part of the package, without the help of the concessions after the aforesaid period. The repayment period for restructured (past) debts should not exceed seven years from the date of implementation of the package. In the case of tiny/decentralised sector units, the period of reliefs/concessions and repayment period of restructured debts which were hitherto, two years and three years respectively have been revised, so as not to exceed five and seven years respectively, as in the case of other SSI units. Based on the norms specified above, it will be for the banks/ financial institutions to decide whether a sick SSI unit is potentially viable or not. Viability of a unit identified as sick, should be decided quickly and made known to the unit and others concerned at the earliest. The rehabilitation package should be fully implemented within six months from the date the unit is declared as 'potentially viable'/'viable'. While identifying and implementing the rehabilitation package, banks/FIs are advised to do 'holding operation' for a period of six months. This will allow small-scale units to draw funds from the cash credit account at least to the extent of their deposit of sale proceeds during the period of such 'holding operation'.

(c) Reliefs and Concessions for Rehabilitation of Potentially Viable Units

(i) It is emphasised that only those units which are considered to be potentially viable should be taken up for rehabilitation. The reliefs and concessions specified are not to be given in a routine manner and have to be decided by concerned bank/financial institution based on the commercial judgment and merits of each case. Banks have also the freedom to extend reliefs and concessions beyond the parameters in deserving cases. Only in exceptional cases, concessions/reliefs beyond the parameters should be considered. In fact, the viability study itself should contain a sensitivity analysis in respect of the risks involved that in turn will enable firming up of the corrective action matrix.

(ii) Units becoming sick on account of wilful mismanagement, wilful default, unauthorized diversion of funds, disputes among partners/promoters, etc. should not be considered for rehabilitation and steps should be taken for recovery of bank's dues. The definition of wilful default, as given by RBI *vide* its Circular DBOD No. BC. DL. (W) 12/20.016.002 (1) 98-99 dated 20th February, 1999, broadly cover the following:

(a) Deliberate non-payment of the dues despite adequate cash flow and good networth.

(b) Siphoning off of funds to the detriment of the defaulting unit.
(c) Assets financed have either not been purchased or have been sold and proceeds have been misutilised.
(d) Misrepresentation/falsification of records.
(e) Disposal/removal of securities without bank's knowledge.
(f) Fraudulent transactions by the borrower.

The views of the lending FI/banks in regard to wilful mismanagement of funds/defaults will be treated as final.

(d) Delegation of Powers

The delay in the implementation of agreed rehabilitation packages should be reduced. One of the factors contributing to such delay was found to be the time taken for obtaining clearance from the Controlling Office for the reliefs and concessions. As it is essential to accelerate the process of clearance, the banks and the financial institutions may delegate sufficient powers to senior officers at various levels such as district, divisional, regional, zonal and also at head office to sanction the bank's or the financial institution's commitment to its share in the rehabilitation package drawn up in conformity with the prescribed guidelines.

(e) Illustrative List of Warning Signals of Incipient Sickness

The following are the list of warning that are thrown up during the Scrutiny of Borrowal Accounts and other Related Records (e.g. Periodical Financial Data, Statements, Report on Inspection of Factory Premises and Godowns, etc.)

(i) Continuous irregularities in cash credit/overdraft accounts such as inability to maintain stipulated margin on continuous basis or drawings frequently exceeding sanctioned limits, periodical interest debited remaining unrealised;

(ii) Outstanding balance in cash credit account remaining continuously at the maximum;
(iii) Failure to make timely payment of instalments of principal and interest on term loans;
(iv) Complaints from suppliers of raw materials, water, power, etc. about non-payment of bills;
(v) Non-submission or undue delay in submission or submission of incorrect stock statements and other control statements;
(vi) Attempts to divert sale proceeds through accounts with other banks;
(vii) Downward trends in credit summations;
(viii) Frequent return of cheques or bills;
(ix) Steep decline in production figures;
(x) Downward trends in sales and fall in profits;
(xi) Rising level of inventories, which may include large proportion of slow or non-moving items;
(xii) Larger and longer outstanding in bill accounts;
(xiii) Longer period of credit allowed on sale documents negotiated through the bank and frequent return by the customers of the same as also allowing large discount on sales;
(xiv) Failure to pay statutory liabilities;
(xv) Utilization of funds for purposes other than running the units.
(xvi) Not furnishing the required information/data on operations in time.
(xvii) Unreasonable/wide variations in sales/receivables levels *vis-à-vis* level of operation of the unit.
(xviii) Non-co-operation for stock inspections, etc.
(xix) Delay in meeting commitments towards payments of instalments due, crystallized liabilities under LC/BGs, etc.
(xx) Diverting/routing of receivables through non-lending banks.

(f) Reliefs and Concessions which can be Extended by Banks/ Financial Institutions to Potentially Viable Sick SSI Units under Rehabilitation

The viability and the rehabilitation of a sick SSI unit would depend primarily on the unit's ability to continue to service its repayment obligations including the past restructured debts. It is, therefore, essential to ensure that ordinarily there is no write off or scaling down of debt such as by reduction in rate of interest with retrospective effect except to the extent indicated in the guidelines. The guidelines on various parameters on reliefs and concessions are given below.

(i) *Interest Dues on Cash Credit and Term Loan*: If penal rates of interest or damages have been charged, such charges should be waived from the accounting year of the unit in which it started incurring cash losses continuously. After this is done, the unpaid interest on term loans and cash credit during this period should be segregated from the total liability and funded. No interest may be charged on funded interest and repayment of such funded interest should be made within a period not exceeding three years from the date of commencement of implementation of the rehabilitation programme.

(ii) Keeping into consideration the above facts and figures, the following strategies has to be adopted for prevention of industrial sickness: Unadjusted interest dues such as interest charged between the date up to which rehabilitation package was prepared and the date from which actually implemented, may also be funded on the same terms as at (i) above.

(iii) *Term Loans*: The rate of interest on term loans may be reduced, where considered necessary, by not more than three per cent in the case of tiny/decentralised sector units and by not more than two per cent for other SSI units, below the document rate.

(iv) After the unadjusted interest portion of the cash credit account is segregated as indicated at (i) and (ii) above, the balance representing principal dues may be treated as irregular to the extent it exceeds drawing power. This amount may be funded as Working Capital Term Loan (WCTL) with a repayment schedule not exceeding 5 years. The rate of interest applicable may be 1.5 per cent to 3 per cent points below the prevailing fixed rate/prime lending rate, wherever applicable, to all sick SSI units including tiny and decentralized units.

(v) *Cash Losses*: Cash losses are likely to be incurred in the initial stages of the rehabilitation programme till the unit reaches the break-even level. Such cash losses excluding interest as may be incurred during the nursing programme may also be financed by the bank or the financial institution, if only one of them is the financier. But if both are involved in the rehabilitation package, the financial institution concerned should finance such cash losses. Interest may be charged on the funded amount at the rates prescribed by SIDBI under its scheme for rehabilitation assistance. Future cash losses in this context will refer to losses from the time of implementation of the package up to the point of cash break-even as projected. Future cash losses as above, should be worked out before interest (i.e., after excluding interest) on working capital, etc., due to the banks and should be financed by the financial institutions if it is one of the financiers of the unit. In other words, the financial institutions should not be asked to provide for interest due to the banks in the computation of future cash losses and this should be taken care of by future cash accruals. The interest due to the bank should be funded by it separately. Where, however, a commercial bank alone is the financier, the future cash losses including interest will be financed by it. The interest on the funded amounts of cash losses/interest will be at the rates prescribed by Small Industries Development Bank of India under its scheme for rehabilitation assistance.

(vi) *Working Capital*: Interest on working capital may be charged at 1.5 per cent below the prevailing fixed/prime lending rate wherever applicable. Additional working capital limits may be extended at a rate not exceeding the PLR.

(vii) *Contingency Loan Assistance*: For meeting escalations in capital expenditure to be incurred under the rehabilitation programme, banks/financial institutions may provide, where considered necessary, appropriate additional financial assistance up to 15 per cent of the estimated cost of rehabilitation by way of contingency loan assistance. Interest on this contingency assistance may be charged at the concessional rate allowed for working capital assistance.

(viii) *Funds for Start-up Expenses and Margin for Working Capital*: There will be need to provide the unit under rehabilitation with funds for start-up expenses (including payment of pressing creditors) or margin money for working capital in the form of long-term loans. Where a financial institution is not involved, banks may provide the loan for start-up expenses, while margin money assistance may either come from SIDBI under its Refinance Scheme for Rehabilitation or should be provided by State Government where it is operating a Margin Money Scheme. Interest on fresh rehabilitation term loan may be charged at a rate 1.5 per cent below the prevailing fixed/prime lending rate wherever applicable or as prescribed by SIDBI/NABARD where refinance is obtained from it for the purpose. All interest rate concessions would be subject to annual review depending on the performance of the units.

(ix) *Promoters' Contribution*: As per the extant RBI guidelines, promoter's contribution towards the rehabilitation package is fixed at a minimum of 10 per cent of the additional long-term requirements under the rehabilitation package in the case of tiny sector units and at 20 per cent of such requirements for other units.

In the case of units in the decentralized sector, promoter's contribution may not be insisted upon. A need is felt for increasing the promoters' contribution towards rehabilitation from the present limits. It is, therefore, open to banks and financial institutions to stipulate a higher promoters' contribution where warranted. At least 50 per cent of the above promoters' contribution should be brought in immediately and the balance within six months. For arriving at promoters' contribution, the monetary value of the sacrifices from banks, financial institutions and Government may be taken into account, in addition to the long-term requirement of funds under the rehabilitation package. While evolving packages, it should be made a pre-condition that the promoters should bring in their contribution within the stipulated time-frame. Further, in regard to concessions and relief made available to sick units, banks should incorporate a 'Right of Recompense' clause in the sanction letter and other documents to the effect that when such units turn the corner and rehabilitation is successfully completed, the sacrifices undertaken by the FIs and banks should be recouped from the units out of their future profits/ cash accruals.

In these regards, the following steps gather immense importance:

(i) Banks and other financial institutions must undertake a careful project appraisal before assisting an industrial unit. At the same time, financial transactions of their clients must be closely monitored by sending questions and information instead of just receiving periodical but outdated returns from them.

(ii) Banks must supervise the assisted units relating to debit and credit balances, forwarding and transferring funds to sister concerns, relatives, etc.

(iii) One or two staff members of the banks and other

financial institutions must be always in charge of periodical inspection of the assisted units so as to ensure its efficiency and proper review of production schedules, stock of raw materials and finished goods.

(iv) Any sort of discrepancies in collecting information or from the unit should not be tolerated. The service of efficient financial analysts must be available to each bank branch at short notice.

(v) As a general rule, banks and other financial institution must nominate directors in the industrial units, more particularly those which are likely to detect sickness.

(vi) Almost care must be taken in financing stocks of raw-materials and finished goods which are often affected by sharp price fluctuations.

(vii) In case of overdrawing, the assisted firms needs to be suggested about its underlying problems and should also be ensured that remedial measures are initiated.

(viii) Banks need to be extra careful when they have to provide large funds to neglected and priority sectors. Such landing should not be at the cost of financial prudence.[2]

4.3 Role of the Government

In a developing country like India, the Government is often a dominant stakeholder even in privately owned enterprises. The various tax relief and subsidies it provides, its ownership or control of the institutions that finances organisations, its enterprises related policies stemming from its overriding concern with industrial development, etc. make it a major stakeholder even in minor enterprises. Its actions often affect the health of whole industries. New units come up through appropriate policies, tax incentives, subsidies, infrastructural facilities, etc. and they also disappear or get sick like a simple magic. The policies of financial and infrastructural support provided or withheld by the government is a determinant of health and sickness of many an industrial unit. Frequent changes in Government policies need to be avoided to reduce industrial sickness.

The Government can play a crucial role by ensuring adequate supply of power, transport and raw materials and taking care that its policies formulated to achieve certain social objectives do not affect the industrial units. The possibilities of creating a fund for the purpose need to be exposed.

Quite often than not, rehabilitation necessitates certain steps on the part of the government. Whenever necessary, it should take quick decision to declare a unit as "Relief undertaking" to prevent creditors from moving the court for winding up, pending rehabilitation. In appropriate cases, the Government has to agree to grant time for payment of arrears of stationery dues by the sick units in planned manner. Prompt action by Government on all matters where on their part is necessary, helps in rehabilitation.[3]

Since the attainment of statehood in 1972, the state Government of Manipur has continuously strived for balanced economic growth through strategies which can offset the geographical disadvantage confronting the State and which can optimise its productive capacities and its vibrant human resource capital. In acknowledgement of the felt need to further pursue attainment of these basic objectives the state Government continues its commitment of policies which can further catalyse growth, reduce social disparity and poverty; create an environment conducive to investment and generate gainful employment especially for entrepreneurs and the educated unemployed.

For fulfilment of these basic objectives, the promotion of rapid industrialisation was a major strategy of the Government. This strategy seeks to integrate industrial promotion efforts with the fast changing national economic scenario in the post-1991 era. Accordingly, the State Government takes due note of the policy initiatives of the Government of India in every sector of economic (industrial, commercial, financial) activity which, *inter alia*, are seeking to:

- Create a liberal investment environment for economic activity especially industrial activity. Minimise Government regulation and control.

- Move towards a supportive role i.e. facilitation.
- Create internationally competitive basic infrastructure facilities.
- Extend preferential treatment to priority sectors of industrial activity through an incentive mechanism.
- Provide full freedom of industrial and commercial activity within clearly established and transparent parameters.

The State Government is aware that while the changing economic and industrial climate in the country has provided freedom to investors and entrepreneurs to set up units for economic/industrial activity according to their own choice, this freedom is more likely to be exercised in favour of geographically advantageous States. Investors/Entrepreneurs are likely to be naturally drawn towards these advantages are coupled with an attractive incentive/subsidy regime which these States offer. In such a situation rapid industrial promotion in Manipur warrants the adoption of a multi-dimensional strategy which depends not only on a subsidy/incentive regime but which optimises the States potential and offsets its disadvantages.

Prior to 1982, planning policy for industrial growth was conducted through specific instructions/order/guidelines. The Industrial Policy of 1982 was the first attempt to co-relate the perception of Government in matters relating to the industrialisation of Manipur. It laid primary emphasis on development of the small scale sector but also gave due attention towards development of large and medium sector industries. In essence, however, both policy initiatives sought to depend mainly on an incentive/subsidy regime. It was expected that this regime would be sufficiently attractive to overcome the lethargy/reluctance of investors and entrepreneurs to consider serious and substantiate investment in Manipur. Consequently, while these policy announcements of the State Government had limited impact on industrial investment and growth, the State has not witnessed the desired level of industrial activity. This is primarily because these policy initiatives have not:

- Created an integrated investor-friendly environment for economic/industrial activity.
- Secured the location and establishment of any Central Public Sector Undertaking which can, in turn, catalyse ancillary units.
- Competed successfully with the subsidy/incentive regime of more advantageous State-this has been a zero-sum game.
- Responded effectively to the need for basic infrastructure facilities, both physical (power, communication, water etc.) and financial (credit linkage/support).
- Ensured optimal development of entrepreneurial skills and utilisation of human resource capital.
- Fully utilised the natural resources/potential/advantage (climate, agro-base, minerals, etc.) of the state.
- Maximised the exploitation of the potential and benefit inherent in Indo-Myanmar Border Trade.
- Enhanced product competitiveness in the domestic/regional/neighbouring market.

In the above background, the State Government was of the firm view that a constructive industrial policy for Manipur must address itself to building on its strength and gains; correction of the distortions and weaknesses that have become apparent; attainment of competitiveness at the national/regional level; enhancement of productivity; creation of congenial environment; and optimal use of natural resources in an eco-compatible manner. The pursuit of new horizons will be tempered by the need to ensure "continuity with change" and the cost-effective use of the State's resources, both financial and natural. All sectors (small, medium or large), whether public/private be encouraged.

In pursuit of the above outlined objective the State Government has initiated to take the following steps by adopting a New Industrial Strategy as detailed below:

I. Creation of an Integrated Investor-Friendly Environment

The State Government recognises that a secured law and order environment is an essential pre-requisite to sustained economic activity. Accordingly, the State Government will not only underline its commitment to providing this environment, but will also set up a special monitoring cell to assess provide the requisite security cover to all major industrial investment in the state.

In order to facilitate investment, the State Government will set up a single-window facilitation/escort mechanism which will seek to provide and or co-ordinate all services and clearance essential for expeditious establishment of an industrial unit.

The State Government will initiate programmes of publicity and investment promotion to familiarise investors with the industrial opportunities available in Manipur.

The State Government will seek an interventionist role of the Central Government in the industrialisation of special category states and canvass for financial assistance for creation of an effective investment environment. In addition, the state will continue to impress upon the Government of India to locate and establish Central Public Sector Undertakings {CPSUs} which can also catalyse the growth of ancillary units.

II. Infrastructural Development Support

The Government of Manipur has decided to take the following steps for infrastructure development for growth and development of industries in the state:

(i) The State Government will adopt an integrated approach to infrastructural support/development. In addition to the upgradation of basic facilities at the Takyelpat, Industrial Estate, the State Government will undertake phases development of the following:

- Integrated Infrastructural Development Centre at Moreh in Chandel district.
- Export Promotion Industrial Park at Kakching in Thoubal district.

- Export Processing Zone at Moreh in Chandel district.
- Industrial Growth Centre at Kanglatongbi in Senapati district.
- Four additional industrial locations viz. Jiribam (Imphal), Litan (Ukhrul), Noney (Tamenglong) and Nambol (Bishnupur) to catalyse balanced dispersal of industries.

(ii) The above-named centres will be provided assured security, water, power, communication and other basic facilities essential to establishment/functioning of industrial units.

(iii) The development of these centres will be compatible with environmental/ecological priorities.

(iv) The State Government will encourage the creation of supportive infrastructure like cold storage, packing house, pre-cooling facilities, refrigeration, etc.

(v) The State Government will accord priority to mobilisation of financial credit/support linkage for industrial projects, particularly in respect of the small scale sector from/through Small Industries Development Bank of India (SIDBI), Manipur Industrial Development Corporation Limited (MANIDCO) and nationalised banks. Support from North Eastern Development Financial Corporation Ltd. (NEDFC) will also be mobilised. The State Government will consider the establishment of a suitable official mechanism to coordinate and facilities the financial needs of industrial units.

III. Maximising Resource Utilisation

(i) Taking note or the state's natural resources and potential the State Government will accord priority to investment in the following:

- Agro-based industries.
- Industries based on locally available raw

materials, including minerals and waste products with local/regional demand.

- All units which take advantage of the Indo-Myanmar Border Trade.
- Handloom and handicrart sector.
- Electronics sector.
- Petro-chemical based industries.
- Forest-based industries not involving depletion of the tree population.
- Export oriented activities/industries.
- All non-polluting, labour intensive units.
- Units using non-conventional energy devices/systems/technology.

(ii) The State Government will promote prospecting, extracting, processing and marketing of mineral resources, chromite, soapstone, serpentinite, idocrase, etc.

(iii) The State Government will accord the status of industry to tourism and provide all admissible incentives/support accordingly.

iv. Competitiveness, Quality Improvement, Skill Upgradation

Upgradation of quality and technology are the prime movers in achieving competitiveness in the domestic market and realising export objectives. With a view to improve the competitiveness of manufacturing units in the small scale sector, a programme for modernisation and upgradation of technology will be implemented. They will cover a package of financial incentives and improvement of training facilities by inviting Central Government Organisations such as Small Industry Service Institute (SISI), National Small Industries Corporation (NSIC) and Department of Electronics (DoE) to set up technology centres, tool rooms and other testing facility.

Special training programmes, implant study, open house discussions/seminars on trading and marketing activities will be organised for export-oriented manufacturing/processing industries.

The State Government will prioritise programmes for development of entrepreneurial skills.

v. Assistance to Sick Industrial Units

The State Government views the problem of industrial sickness with concern and will endeavour to assist sick industries that can be revived. The State Government has already initiated a detailed programme for rehabilitation of sick public sector undertaking. The possibility of converting these into a joint sector unit in collaboration with private partners will be explored and given priority; failing which privatisation will be considered.

For the small sector unit, a cell in the Directorate of Commerce and Industries will be opened to monitor the sick units, initially, a survey of the existing small scale units in the state will be carried out to categorise these units according to their potential for revival. Based on this survey a package of policy measures will be initiated to make these sick units viable, wherever cost-effective.

vi. Promotion of Indo-Myanmar Border Trade

The State Government will take positive steps to optimise the advantages offered by the opening of the border trade with Myanmar at Moreh in Chandel district.

An Export Cell of the Directorate of Commerce and Industries will be the Nodal Agency which, *inter alia,* will:

- educate, train and guide traders/entrepreneurs in international trading.
- conduct an export potential survey.
- undertake measures to promote trade-motivated industrial activity.
- optimise use of agricultural/horticultural/forest resources across the border facilitate setting up of trade centres with integrated and in-house basic facilities.

The New Industrial Policy of Manipur, 2002 has also laid the following missions, goals and strategy for the development of industrial economy of the state and avoiding industrial sickness:

Mission

To facilitate rapid and substantial industrial development in the State through enhanced investment, an investor-friendly environment, provision for infrastructure and institutional support, attractive incentive package and optimum utilisation of existing resources shall be created in order to gainfully exploit emerging opportunities in the National and International markets and generate substantial income and employment avenues for the people of Manipur. This will be done by providing industry access to high quality infrastructure, extending institutional support for technology upgradation, deregulating the business environment for an efficient, proactive and transparent administrative framework and catalysing the entrepreneurial as well as creative capabilities of the human resources.

Goal

(a) Create necessary conditions for maximum possible utilisation by tapping locally available raw-material and human resources for industrialisation.

(b) Create gainful employment opportunities for local population.

(c) Develop industrial infrastructure in selected areas by providing common facilities in a compact area for specialised categories of industrial units. Provide other critical infrastructure such as power, water, communication, etc.

(d) Promote export-oriented industries with a view to exploit the emerging market opportunities in the neighbouring countries.

(e) Develop marketing facilities for industrial products.

(f) Encourage large and medium industries in public,

private, joint and assisted sectors to create an industrial base making use of the available resource base of the State in selective categories compatible with local environment and ecology.

(g) Develop Village and Small Scale Service and Business Enterprises (SSSBE) to provide self-employment to educated youths.
(h) Develop and promote tourism industry in the State.
(i) Revive and rehabilitate sick industrial units in the State.
(j) Develop food processing industry by facilitating forward and backward linkages.
(k) Expedite formalisation and development of cross border trade with Myanmar.
(l) Provide investor-friendly environment by removing procedural bottlenecks and legal hurdles.
(m) Provide industry access to high quality infrastructure.
(n) Enhance value addition in products and processes through rapid technology upgradation.
(o) Encouraging quality control, standardisation and competitiveness of the local products.
(p) Ensuring minimisation of pollution and encouraging eco-friendly units.
(q) Encouraging industry based on medicinal plants and encouraging research and development in the field.

Strategy

(a) Take effective steps to promote industrial culture and create a secure environment for entrepreneurs.
(b) Expedite completion of the on-going Growth Centre and Export Promotion Industrial Park (EPIP) projects and take measures to revitalise the existing Industrial Estates.
(c) Create quality industrial infrastructure in compact areas such as Integrated Infrastructure Development Centre, Food Parks, Information Technology Parks, Bio-technology Parks, Cold Storage Chains and Warehousing, etc.

(d) Enhance availability of other critical infrastructure such as power, water and communication for industrial use.
(e) Create Industrial Facilitation Committees with the mandate to provide single window clearance to Small Scale Industrial Units, Large and Medium Industrial Units. Adopt the same framework at the District level.
(f) Identify thrust areas for attracting investment keeping in view the comparative advantages of the State.
(g) Provide necessary infrastructure at identified International Trade points in the State. Expedite operationalisation and upgradation of the Trading points.
(h) Strengthen the network of training institutions in the State and create quality training facilities in sophisticated and specialised trades by encouraging investment in such facilities by the Government of India, the State Government and the private sector.
(i) Provide liberal support to training of the entrepreneurs.
(j) Strengthen the role of MANIDCO as the premier promoter of large and medium scale industries by extending suitable financial and policy support to it.
(k) Provide an incentive package of subsidies and concession over and above the incentive available in the Central Government's North-East Industrial Policy, 1997 and other concessions so as to attract substantial private establishment in the State.
(l) Devise a suitable self-employment scheme for unemployed youths to set up new ventures in service, small business and tiny manufacturing sectors.
(m) Facilitate credit availability from the banks and other financial institutions for promoting industrial activity.
(n) Accelerate exploration of mines and minerals for enhancing the resources base of the State.
(o) Take effective steps to promote handloom and handicrafts sector by providing, *inter alia*, marketing access to handloom and handicrafts produce through MHHDC and other means.
(p) To develop tourism industry and provide necessary support available to other industrial activity.
(q) Revive potentially viable sick State PSUs by taking

effective steps including privatisation and, close down unviable sick PSUs.

(r) Adoption of broad policy or Foreign Direct Investment (FDI) and joint venture proposals.

The following steps may also be undertaken by the Government to avoid industrial sickness:

(i) Government departments and other public sector undertakings should not withhold the payment of the bills of SSI units for an unduly long time. If withhold, it causes liquidity problems to the SSI units, adversely affecting their production cycle, which may culminate in their sickness.

(ii) Further, the Government may defer the recovery of statutory dues like duty, sales tax, etc., from the sick units, which may be paid by them after their rehabilitation, in suitable instalments, without interest or penalty.

(iii) Frequent changes in the taxation laws and Government policies also adversely affect the units in the small scale sector. The Government should, therefore, exercise due care in such matters to safeguard the interest of the small scale sector.

(iv) The small scale sector usually faces the problem of scarcity of raw materials. The government may, therefore, arrange for the supply of scarce raw materials through some government agencies, on quota basis, commensurate with the scale of operation of the units. Preference should be given to the smaller of the SSI units.

(v) While resorting to load-shedding of power supply, the Government may adopt a liberal attitude towards the small scale sector so that their production may not get adversely affected.

(vi) Small scale industrial units are required to deal with many inspectors and officers from various Government departments and agencies like excise and customs, Bureau of Indian Standards, factory inspectors, fire brigade, municipal sanitary department, etc. They are also required to submit several *pro forma* to different Government authorities, and to meet the provisions of various laws and rules passed from time to time.

In this regard, it is suggested that one comprehensive *pro forma* should be designed, incorporating all the relevant informations required to be submitted by the SSI units, copies whereof may be sent to all the authorities concerned, for information and control purposes. The number of such authorities should be kept at the minimum level. Further, all the laws and rules, relevant to the small sector, should be codified in one volume, which the small entrepreneurs may easily comprehend and follow.

These measures would substantially reduce the extend of their confusion and harassment and they would be able to utilise their time and energy, so saved, for more productive purposes, for the profitability and progress of their unit.

(vii) Law and order problems needs to be tackled properly by the Government so that there is a conducive atmosphere for the entrepreneurs to run their businesses without any hindrances.

4.4 Role of the Entrepreneur

In fact, it is the sole responsibility of the concerned entrepreneur to avert sickness in the unit set up by him. This can be possible if the entrepreneur does his job properly while preparing his project work, if he understands and pays adequate attention to the deficiencies pointed out by the aspiring officials of the banks other financial institutions, if he selects the required capital goods carefully, if he appoints only the efficient and required number of workers in time, if he implements his project within his estimated cost and as per time schedule.

There are different stages to bring out by the management in the process of winning around the sick units; management change stage, evaluation stage, emergency stage, stabilization stage and the return of normal growth stage.[3]

In the first stage, change in the top management is needed where there is sickness due to their wrong decision in the business set up and subsequent failure to recognize the problem and take preventive steps. However, this type of change may not be applicable to small proprietary concern. For the cases, change in management means a change in heart, a new thrust or an ability to take tough decision to have their business.[4]

The second next stage is the evaluation stage where the management has to find out the possible viability of the firm and prepare a re-organisation plan. The various roles played by the management in this stage are as follows:

(i) Concentration of greatest efforts on the determined area so as to get the greatest average and to develop plan accordingly.

(ii) Focusing more on generating cash inflows because most of the sick units at this stage have negative cash flows.

(iii) Review of credit policy so as to avail longer credit period and granting shorter credit period.

(iv) Downsizing of excessive manpower and segmentation of business into segments; production-wise or operation-wise and judge their contribution to the firm's profitability so that unprofitable segments with negative cash generations may be dropped.

(v) Evaluation of all these segments by means of SWOT (Strength, Weakness, Opportunity and Threat) analysis with a view to capitalise on strength and opportunities and minimize on weakness and threats.

(vi) Disposing of all loosing segments so as to strengthen the cash position of the existing segments.

(vii) Communication of these plans to all concerned.

The next stage is the stage of stabilization. During this stage, the emphasis shifts to a three-pronged strategy[5]. They are:

(i) concentration on profitability in addition to cash flow

(ii) run existing operation better, and

(iii) reposturing the firm to provide a sound platform for medium term growth.

There are also other stages which need to be implemented when things are improved. Introduction of a control system is the need of the hour. One of the important reasons of industrial sickness in our country was due to lack of such a system in the past.

4.5 The Role of Professionals

Professionals such as financial analysts, project coordinators, accountants, etc. has a big role to play in checking and signalling the industrial sickness through continuous study adopting different models for forecasting of sickness. It should be the joint efforts of accountants, engineers, marketing personnels and production people to avoid sickness and even if so happens, for revival of sick units. But in a small state like Manipur, small entrepreneurs cannot bear the cost of such professionals. In order to overcome such a problem, the State Government should make a provision to establish consultancy cells in banks, other financial institutions, District Industry Centres and other Government Departments, consisting of professional in different fields of industrial operations. This will help in smooth functioning of industrial units and at the same time, helps in preventing and revival of the sick unit by closely monitoring the implementation of rehabilitation package.

References

1. Reddy, K.C., "*Sickness in Small Scale Industries*" Ashish Publishing House, New Delhi, 1983, p. 85.
2. Simha, S.L.N. (Ed.) "*Industrial Sickness: Role of Banks,*" "*Credit Management (Planning, Appraisal and Supervision)*", Institute for Financial Management, Madras, 1978, pp. 429-431.
3. Chakraborty, S.K. and Sen, P.K. (edited): "*Industrial Sickness and Revival in India – Essays, Cases and Debates*" IIM, Calcutta, 1980, p. 59.

4. Srilakshim, M. "*Topical Review of Industrial Sickness*". Part-I, SIET, Sept., 1980. pp. 3-4.
5. Sahu, P.K., 'Some Conceptual Issues on Industrial Sickness." *Indian Journal of Commerce*, March, 1985, Vol. XXXVII, Part No. 142, p. 21.

5

Findings and Suggestions of the Study

In this chapter, the findings and suggestions of the whole study are presented.

Findings of the Study

The findings of the study are discussed as hereunder:

5.1 Year of Commencement of Unit

It has been found that 36 per cent of the total sampled units had started their business from the year 1995-2000, followed by 32 per cent in the year 2000-05. Only 12 per cent started commencing their business in the year 1990-95. The maximum sampled units of Bishnupur, Senapati, Tamenglong, Ukhrul, Chandel and Churachandpur districts were newly commenced units as compared to Imphal East, Imphal West and Thoubal districts.

5.2 Age of Entrepreneurs

56 per cent of the total entrepreneurs whose units became sick started their units at the age of 31-40 years followed by 34 per cent at the age of 21-30 years. Only 10 per cent started at the age of 41-50 years. District-wise, Tamenglong, Bishnupur and Ukhrul district had maximum number of sick units that had been started by entrepreneurs in the age group of 31-40 years.

Very few started in the age-group of 41-50 years in all the districts.

5.3 Form of Organisation

Maximum of the sampled units are proprietorship form of organization (80.0%), followed by partnership firms (12.0%). Among the districts, Churachandpur, Senapati, Bishnupur and Imphal East districts had only the proprietorship form of organization in the sampled unit. In other words, it can be concluded that proprietorship form of organization is the most common form of organization in the state.

5.4 Type of Industries

It is interesting to note that maximum of the sampled units are food based industries (26.0%), followed by metal based (16.0%) and handlooms and handicrafts and automobile and engineering units (14.0% each). The food based industries sampled are mostly concentrated in Imphal West district (23.1%), Thoubal, Bishnupur and Ukhrul districts (15.4 % each). As far as metal based industries are concerned, they are evenly distributed in all the districts except in Imphal East district. It is quite interesting to note that there are no sick handlooms and handicrafts industries in Imphal West, Ukhrul and Churachandpur districts as far as the sampled units are concerned.

5.5 Educational Background of Entrepreneurs

Educational background of the entrepreneurs also played an important role in the success or failure of a unit. It has been found after the study that 26 per cent each of under-matriculation, under-graduation and graduation formed the number of such entrepreneur whose units had became sick. Matriculation formed 20 per cent whereas, it is worthwhile to mention that post-graduation formed only 2 per cent.

Among the districts, entrepreneurs who were not

matriculates are found in all the districts except in Imphal East and Imphal West districts. The only post-graduated entrepreneurs were found in the Imphal West District. Again, the maximum of graduated entrepreneurs are found in the Imphal West district (42.6%).

5.6 Professional Experience of Entrepreneurs

It is learnt that professional experience of the entrepreneurs had nothing to do in the process of industrial sickness. 70 per cent of the concerned entrepreneurs had the unit related professional experience. Even among the nine districts of the state, the majority of them had the required professional experience. With all the required professional experience, the causes of sickness were such that their units became sick and had to close down units for some of them.

5.7 Generation of Entrepreneurs

78 per cent of the total sampled entrepreneurs are first generation entrepreneurs. Further, entrepreneurs hailing from Imphal East, Bishnupur and Chandel districts are all first generation entrepreneurs. Quite interestingly, 60 per cent of Tamenglong district is second generation entrepreneurs. Again, it can be noted that there is no third generation entrepreneurs among the sampled units. In other words, maximum number of entrepreneurs had professional experience in their related field, but they are fresh in their own practical field of entrepreneurship.

5.8 Feasibility Study

Out of the total 50 entrepreneurs, only 21 (42.0%) conducted the feasibility study before commencement of their units. Quite surprisingly, none of the Thoubal and Senapati district entrepreneurs had conducted any sort of feasibility study. The same pattern continues in the case of Bishnupur, Tamenglong, Ukhrul and Chandel districts where maximum of the sampled entrepreneurs didn't conduct any study (more than 60.0%). It is very interesting to note that, in case of Imphal East district, all of the entrepreneurs had undertaken the feasibility study.

It has been further found that 8 out of 21 (38.1%) conducted the study by themselves whereas the remaining 13 took the help of other agencies like SBI, SISI, AMEA, DIC etc. for conducting the said study.

District-wise also, entrepreneurs hailing from Imphal East, Tamenglong, Chandel had entrusted the job of feasibility study with other experienced body. It can also be noted that all the entrepreneurs who had undertaken feasibility study in Thoubal district believed in themselves as far as the study was concerned.

5.9 Entrepreneurship Development Programme

26 (52.0%) of the total 50 sampled entrepreneurs attended EDP, conducted by various agencies. District-wise, Imphal West District had the maximum number of such entrepreneurs (16.0%) followed by Imphal East District (10.0%) and Churachandpur District (6.0%).

It is worthwhile to mention that it is the Imphal East district that all the sampled entrepreneurs had attended such entrepreneurial development programmes. But, majority of the Thoubal, Bishnupur, Senapati, Tamenglong, Ukhrul and Chandel districts entrepreneurs didn't consider it necessary to attend EDPs for their smooth running of their units. Very interestingly, SBI conducted majority of the EDPs followed AMEA and DIC.

5.10 Financing Pattern of Units

Finance is a highly versatile resource which demands proper utilization and planning. Financial discipline, information, forecasting, planning and control have a high profile in industrial management. In fact, the availability of enough finance is the most important factor, without it, the idea to start business or industry will always remain a simple wish.

Even if the necessary finance is available, there are many obstacles in financing the small scale industries. These obstacles are always rated as high risks. In fact, the risk element is present in every industrial financing.

(i) District-wise Pattern of Financing

Regarding the average loan taken, the entrepreneurs hailing from Imphal West, Chandel, Imphal East and Ukhrul districts have taken more loan than those from Thoubal, Senapati, Tamenglong, Bishnupur and Churachandpur districts.

Quite interestingly, the hill districts of Ukhrul, Chandel and Churachandpur far exceed the other districts of the state as far as repayment of loans is concerned.

(ii) Form of Organisation-wise Pattern of Financing

The average loan taken by partnership firms far more exceeds the overall average of loan taken by the sampled units. Quite interestingly, on the other hand, the percentage of loan repayment is more for the partnership firms as compared to proprietorship form of organisation.

(iii) Generation-wise Pattern of Financing

The first generation entrepreneurs have taken more financial help than their other counterparts, which is even more than the overall average loan taken by the sampled units. But as regards to the habit of repayment of loan taken, these first generation entrepreneurs are still lagging behind the second generation entrepreneurs.

(iv) Industry-wise Pattern of Financing

The average loan taken by the plastic and rubber based industries is more than double of the overall average loan taken by the sampled units. It is followed by food based and automobile and engineering units. But if compared with the rate of loan repayment, metal based and others' type of industries picture is far better than food based (only 13.24%), wood based (9.62%) and automobile and engineering units (9.28%).

5.11 District-wise Internal Causes of Sickness

40 per cent of the total sick units (20 units) had been caused by internal financial problems. It is followed by faulty project selection (24.0%) and marketing problems (20%). Even among the districts studied, 80 per cent (4 units) of Senapati district suffered from financial problems, followed by 60 per cent each of the Imphal East, Chandel and Churachandpur districts. But, it is very surprising that sick units of Tamenglong and Ukhrul districts had no internal financial problems as compared to other districts. And as far as internal causes of sickness are concerned, it is found that there is no personnel problem in the units studied for industrial sickness.

5.12 District-wise External Problems Relating to Banks and other Financial Institutions

It has been found that 38 per cent (19 units) of all the sick units under study suffered from the severe problem of delay in disbursement of loans by banks and other financial institutions. Delay in detecting early symptoms of sickness (20.0%) and delay in decision and action to rehabilitate the unit (18.0%) also affected the units at their troublesome days of sickness. It was also an interesting scene where 8.0 per cent (4 units) of the sampled units had expressed an external problem due to over-financing by the banks. As far as under-financing is concerned, Imphal East district suffered the most (37.5%) followed by Imphal West district.

5.13 District-wise Sickness made by Government

From the study it has been found that 58 per cent of the total sampled units suffered from red-tapism by government officers

(29 units). No doubt, change in government policies was also a major factor (26.0%) as far as industrial sickness is concerned. In Senapati, Tamenglong and Ukhrul districts, red-tapism played the major role for industrial sickness. It was only an exception in Chandel District. Delay in payment of bills by government departments was a major cause of sickness in Thoubal district as compared to other districts.

5.14 District-wise External Problems

Maximum of the sampled units (38.0%) faced the problem of power as the external problem which is beyond their control. They had to avail power generators, thereby increasing the costs of products. 28 per cent of the units opined marketing as the major external problem as against finance problem (18.0%) and raw-materials (16.0%).

District-wise, power problems (40.0%) and marketing problems (30.0%) had caused as external problems responsible for industrial sickness in Imphal West district. But, finance problem played a major role (60.0%) in Senapati district for industrial sickness. It is worthwhile to mention that raw-materials are plenty in Churachandpur district for industrial development but marketing problem (60.0%) and power problem (40.0%) played major role for industrial sickness.

5.15 District-wise other External Problems

Social problems like strikes, bandhs, insurgents, extortions, etc. are the acute external problems faced by the units. Economic blockades are so common on the two National Highways of Manipur. That's why it is not surprising to note that all the sample units, irrespective of its location, had expressed its uneasiness to cope up with all these external problems.

Given the increasing insurgency problems in the state, outside entrepreneurs (innovative entrepreneurs) are hesitant to come to the insurgency stricken state for establishing their industrial units. These external problems have its long lasting implications for the industrial and overall development of the state.

5.16 District-wise Rehabilitation Package

It is very surprising to note that till date, the state government or any financial institution has not yet declared a unit as sick unit in Manipur. So, there is no question of rehabilitation package in the state. Some of the sampled units have tried to convince the concerned banks, Industries Department and even the state government to declare their units as sick units under the umbrella of All Manipur Entrepreneurs Assn. (AMEA) till date, the concerned authorities are not taking up the required formalities of declaration of sick units and hence, no package of rehabilitation for these units.

5.17 Organisation-wise Internal Causes of Sickness

Financial problems played a major role (43.2%) for industrial sickness in units which are run as sole proprietorship, followed by faulty project selection (22.7%) and marketing problems (20.5%). In the case of partnership firms under study, faulty project selection and production problems (33.3 % each) were equally responsible for industrial sickness as internal causes.

5.18 Organisation-wise External Problems Relating to Banks and other Financial Institutions

Proprietorship form of industrial units had suffered maximum from delay in disbursement of loans (38.6%), followed by under-financing and delay in decision and action to rehabilitate the units (18.2% each). But, it is very noteworthy that partnership firms had no problem with under-financing and over-financing by banks. It was delay in detecting early symptoms of sickness (50.0%) that resulted into sickness for the partnership firms, followed by delay in disbursement of loans (33.3%).

5.19 Organisation-wise Sickness made by Government

Red-tapism by government officers was also an important cause of sickness being faced by the sampled units irrespective of their forms of organization. It was noted after the study that 56.8 per cent of proprietorship and 66.7 per cent of partnership firms faced this problem and referred to it as the major cause of sickness made by Government. Other than this, change in Government policies also affected 27.3 per cent (12 units) of the proprietorship units in the process of becoming sick units.

5.20 Organisation-wise External Problems

36.4 per cent of proprietorship units and 50 per cent of partnership firms had suffered the problems of power scarcity as external problem. Furthermore, marketing problems of proprietorship units are also acute as it affected 31.8 per cent of the said units. Financial problems had also played an adverse role for the partnership firms. But, it is interesting to note that partnership firms had no problem as regards to marketing of its products.

5.21 Industry-wise Internal causes of Sickness

Contrary to plastics and rubber, printing and stationery and automobile and engineering industries, food based industries, faced marketing problems (46.2%) as the main internal cause of sickness. The financial problems also caused serious problems for food based industries (30.8%).

As compared to this, faulty project selection and finance problems affected adversely on automobile and engineering industries (42.9% each). Maximum of the handlooms and handicrafts industries (42.9%) also suffered from financial problems. But, it is interesting to note that production problems had been a major internal problem to metal based industries (37.5%) than to other types of industries.

5.22 Industry-wise External Problems Relating to Banks and other Financial Institutions

Maximum of the food based industries suffered from delay in disbursement of loans (38.5%). On the other hand, it was under-financing by banks that had adversely affected plastics and rubber based industries (75.0%). In the case of automobile and engineering industries, the main problem was delay in disbursement of loans (57.1%) and delay in decision and action to rehabilitate the unit (28.6%). It is also noteworthy that maximum of the units found to be over-financed by banks are food based (50.0%), handlooms and handicrafts (25.0%) and automobile and engineering units (25.0%).

5.23 Industry-wise Sickness made by Government

Majority of the food based industries highlighted red-tapism by Government officers as the major cause of sickness made by Government (69.2%). Not surprisingly, red-tapism alone was the only cause of sickness made by Government for wood based industries.

On the other hand, change in Government policies had also affected adversely to food based and handlooms and handicrafts industries (23.1 % each). But for the plastics and rubber based industries, it was delay in payment of bills by Government departments that became a major cause of industrial sickness made by government (50.0%).

5.24 Industry-wise External Problems

All the industrial units had suffered from power problem since a long-time. But, as have been found from the study that food based industries suffered the most (26.3%), followed by metal based (21.1%) and automobile and engineering (15.8%) industries. Again, raw-materials problems seem to be acute for food based industries (50.0%), followed by metal based industries (25.0%). Industry-wise, marketing problems of handlooms and handicrafts industries was noteworthy while it has no raw-material problem.

Over and above the foregoing causes, it was found from the field survey that most of the sampled units lack financial discipline and information and hardly have they resorted to financial planning and forecasting with no long term prospective in mind. One hardly comes across among the units preparing cash flow statement. If any authority even wanted to rehabilitate these sick units, the financial statements of the units have to be analysed. But in its absence, the process itself is big problem.

Suggestions of the Study

At the very outset, it has to be said that a strong determination is needed for dealing with the disease of industrial sickness. Otherwise, the same disease is definitely bound to spread to the whole industrial sector. In a state like Manipur where resources are very scarce, every effort should be made for its maximum utilization and the question of resources being kept idle and unproductive should not be tolerated. Otherwise, the ever increasing incidence of industrial sickness may threaten the whole socio-economic set up of the state in particular and the country in general.

The following suggestions are made to prevent and avoid industrial sickness in Manipur.

5.25 Suggestions to the Government

(i) A separate cell especially for the sick units needs to be set up in the Department of Commerce and Industries, Government of Manipur. In fact, no one from the concerned department helped the researcher regarding the identification of sick units in the State. Some of the employees even argued that there is not even a single sick unit in the state. Officially, it may be true because no unit as such has been declared as sick in the State of Manipur so far. But a simple visit at the sampled units will understand how the units are running in sick condition or were closed down due to sickness.

(ii) There should be a scientific inventory of the resources available in the state with the object of optimum and sustainable utilization of the resources. One should be in touch with the emerging pattern of demand in and outside Manipur. If we have established comparative advantage over other states in the production of commodities for any type of market, every possible measure should be taken to capitalize on that advantage.

(iii) The growth of small-scale industries is essential both for employment and balanced growth of the economy. The Government should come forward with a policy package consisting of technology, finance and market information. The essence of globalization is that one can have access to market anywhere in the world provided the information is available. The existing Directorate of Industries and Commerce should be given additional responsibility to disseminate the required information in-time, so that our small scale entrepreneurs can capitalize on their advantages.

(iv) Infusion of modern technology in the traditional industries of the state, for example handloom and handicraft industries is a must, to make our industries commercially viable. Advanced technology will reduce the cost of production and will make the export of such products competitive.

(v) So far we have been importing most of the items both from the mainland and Myanmar. There is a talk for establishing a Trans-National Highway, linking the South East Asian Countries with India. Manipur also is on the route of such a Highway. The Government should give a serious thought to the prospects of our industries *vis-à-vis* the markets of the South East Asian Countries. Instead of serving as a station for export and import, we should establish industries in the state, which can cater to foreign demand. This will enable us to reap more benefits from trade. The price competitiveness of Indian goods produced in Manipur and then exported to Myanmar cannot be denied.

(vi) Myanmar is one of the main exporters of rice, pulses and beans. If these commodities are imported freely into the state, it can make these items substantially cheaper in the local market. With this cheap and assured sort of supply, the state can concentrate on the production of high-valued crops and also in agro-processing industries. Similarly teak and precious stones are abundantly available in Myanmar. Carpentry industries based on imported teak from Myanmar and gems industries have substantial scope. There is a huge demand for teak furniture in big cities of India. There is a huge export market for gems and jewellery. What is needed is a careful examination of the export-import activities along the border. The current restrictive perspective of Indo-Myanmar border trade arises from the fact that it is under the purview of the Ministry of Home Affairs, Government of India. This should be transferred to the Ministry of Commerce, Government of India.

(vii) So far we have not been able to produce an entrepreneur class committed to sustained economic growth based on industrialization. The available entrepreneurial training facilities have been unable to remove this bottleneck. In this context, it is imperative that the Government examine scientifically the factors underlying this crisis. Packages that have proved effective in different economic environments need not have similar impact. It needs more internationalisation of the training packages. Lack of finance is not the only factor. The Government should train the entrepreneurs to have a realistic perspective of the international market so that they can capitalize on available comparative advantage anywhere in the world. Their vision needs to be reoriented to realize that smallness of the market is no longer a constraint.

(viii) Trade is a way of life, particularly so in the context of globalization. Instead of resisting it, the Government should try to reap the maximum benefit out of it. The general people's active participation in trade based on the principle of comparative advantage will help in making a positive contribution to the process of economic development in India as Manipur is physically and financially dependent on the mainland. Transfers from the Central Government have been the main stay of the state's fiscal health. The state's internal resource mobilization can finance at the most one month's public expenditure. This characteristic will disappear when the state have a vibrant economy linked to the international market. The question of preservation of culture and identities need to be viewed in a dynamic sense.

(ix) Both the Central and State Governments should first assess and declare those units suffering from this disease as sick units and try to rehabilitate them for the welfare of the state as a whole.

(x) Central as well as State Government needs to give more emphasis on giving wide publicity so as to reach the information to all entrepreneurs regarding any policies or schemes for the development of small scale industries.

(xi) Efforts should be made to strengthen agencies like District Industries Centres (DIC), Manipur Industrial Development Corporation (MANIDCO), and Industrial Training Institute (ITI) to provide necessary facilities like subsidies, grants, tax concessions, training etc. for sick units. Malpractices, at the same time must be prevented at any cost.

(xii) Uninterrupted supply of power should be ensured as it is the most important problem being faced by all the sick units.

(xiii) The SSI units should operate in the areas reserved for them so as to reduce the competition from other sectors. At the same time, the Government should ensure that more number of items be reserved for the exclusive production of the SSI sector.

(xiv) Similarly on the lines of BIFR at the national level, institution at the state level needs to be set up to arbitrate on the declaration of sick units and to approve revival package for SSI units as well as for the state public enterprises.

(xv) Construction of cheap and better industrial sheds for the industrial units needs to be encouraged in order to avoid heavy initial investment in construction of sheds and make projects cost-effective.

(xvi) The Government should establish special institutions to finance industries especially for sick units as in the case of Japan. This is particularly important because even then the commercial banks are providing finance to this sector significantly, they fail to meet the growing need for working capital simply as a result of their liquidity and profitability criteria which are essential for bankers.

(xvii) The State Government, with the help of the Reserve Bank of India should lay down the criteria for dealing with the sick industrial units so that they gets a uniform treatment regarding financial assistance and rehabilitation package.

(xviii) The State Government should take proper and speedy steps to revive the viable units which have fallen sick in the state. A mechanism also needs to be formulated for looking into the sickness of those industrial units which have not availed any assistance from banks.

(xix) Time limit should be prescribed for the DIC to complete the pre-production formation. In other words, the entrepreneur should be saved for running from pillar to post. For achieving this, single-window-system may be introduced both at the state as well as district levels. It is a fact that District Industries Centres (DICs) which were designed to serve this purpose have not achieved it fully. From registration of the unit to preparing feasibility reports, obtaining finance, starting production and marketing the products, the concerned DIC needs to help the entrepreneur in all respects.

(xx) Social problems like strikes, bandhs etc. are creating a big problem for these industrial units as can be found from the field survey. So, proper atmosphere needs to be created where industrial activity is left free out of any disturbances so that economic prosperity and growth can be achieved in this state. Government also needs to provide all kinds of security to the industrial units for its smooth functioning.

5.26 Suggestions to the Banks and other Financial Institutions

(i) Banks and financial institutions should ensure the free flow of funds/credit to the industrial units. But, it should be need-based and not security or target oriented lending.

(ii) Project appraisals should include a thorough appraisal of the project as well as that of the entrepreneurs with regard to their efficiency, sincerity and integrity.

(iii) Delay in disbursement of term loans should be avoided for minimizing delay in the implementation of projects. Maintenance of minimum time-limit for the security of application of loans and sanctioning of loans must be set for all banks and other financial institutions.

(iv) Persons with high integrity and experience in the field of industrial sickness should mean the financial institutions and there must be periodical field visits and interaction with the entrepreneurs. Appreciation of problems of industrial units by concerned officials will pave a way of cordial atmosphere for industrial development.

(v) Once an industrial unit has acquired the symptoms of sickness and the same is reported by the concerned unit or noticed by the financial institute, the concerned institute should conduct a diagnostic study to detect the causes of symptoms and it should be initiated without any delay.

(vi) After the diagnostic study, the financial institution should try to help the entrepreneur for initiating preventive measures without any delay.

(vii) If the unit has already become sick, the viability study of the unit should be conducted without any delay.

(viii) A decision for or against the rehabilitation of units should be taken without any delay on the basis of the outcome of viability study. If it is viable, a comprehensive rehabilitation package should be implemented for the revival of units instead of resorting to some *ad hoc* measures. RBI and IDBI have already issued various guidelines in this regard.

(ix) Screening process for the selection of right person with right project must be properly devised. It can be seen, nowadays, that any project report of any type, specifications are available from consultations and others in the market against payment. The entrepreneurial qualities of the person, other than his project and economic status is more important while deciding to provide financial support to entrepreneurs.

5.27 Suggestions to the Entrepreneurs

(i) A proper project planning with prior feasibility study is a must for staring a unit.

(ii) A first generation entrepreneur should not go in for a large investment in the initial stage.

(iii) Employment of latest techniques of production, skilled labour will help a entrepreneur in the improvement of quality of product and its marketing.

(iv) An entrepreneur should, atleast, acquire entrepreneurial skills in the field of finance, working, production, etc. from management institutions like ICM, AMEA or SISI before starting a unit. This will go a long way in the prevention of with from sickness.

(v) Proper books of account need to be maintained. It is found from the field survey that almost none of them maintained it properly. Statutory obligation may be imposed so that their books of account are prepared and maintained by professional accountants.

(vi) Severe penalties must be levied on entrepreneurs misusing funds or otherwise seeking financial assistance by underhand hands. Preventive measures of sickness should be taken to provide a check on the malpractices of units.

(vii) An individual must have certain values and traits to be a successful entrepreneur. At the same time, it is also a fact that everyone cannot be successful entrepreneurs.

Bibliography

A. Books and Research Works

Agarwal, A.N. (1994): "*Growth and Industrial Origin, Indian Economy – Problems, Development and Planning* ", Vishwa Prakash, New Delhi.

Agarwal, V.K. (1975) : "*Initiative Enterprise and Economic Choices in India*", Munshiram Manoharlal Publishers Pvt. Ltd., New Delhi.

Ahmed, Nissar, (1987): "*Small Scale and Cottage Industries*", Deep & Deep Publications, New Delhi.

Akhouri, M.M.P. and S.V.S.(1978): "*Small Entrepreneurship Development in North Eastern India*" Hyderabad, SIET.

Bidani, S.N. and Mitra P.K. (1982): "*Industrial Sickness – Identification & Rehabilitation*", Vision Books, Delhi.

Balkrishnan, G. (1961): "*Financing of Small Scale Industries in India: 1950-52*", Asia Publishing House, Bombay.

Batra, G.S. and Daugal, R.C. (2000): "*Entrepreneurship and Small Scale Industries*" Deep & Deep Publications Pvt. Ltd., New Delhi.

Berna, J.J. (1960): "*Industrial Entrepreneurship in Madras State*", Asia Publishing House, Bombay.

Bhagwari Jugolish (1966): "*The Economics of Underdeveloped Countries*", World University Library, London.

Bhatia, B.S. and Batra, G.S. (2000): "*Entrepreneurship and Small Business Management*" Deep & Deep Publications Pvt. Ltd., New Delhi.

– – (1997): "*Management of Sick Industries*" Deep & Deep Publications, New Delhi.

Bhattacharya, S.N., (1986): *"Development of Small Scale and Cottage Industries"* Metropolitan Book Co., New Delhi.

Cantillon, Richard, (1971): *"Entrepreneurship and Economic Development"*, The Free Press, New York.

Cashin, P. & R. Sahay, (1996): *"Regional Economic Growth and Convergence in India"*, Finance and Development, IMF, March.

Chakraborty, S.K. and Sen, P.K. (Ed) (1980): *"Industrial Sickness and Revival in Indian-Essays, Cases and Debates"* IIM, Calcutta.

Desai, Vasant, (2000): *"Small Scale Industries and Entrepreneuship"*, Himalaya Publishing House, Mumbai.

— — (2002): *"Dynamics of Entrepreneurial Development and Management"* Himalaya Publishing House, Mumbai.

Deshpande, M.U. (1979): *"Small Scale Industrial Entrepreneurship in a Developing Region"*, Maharashtra, Marathwada University.

Dutta, Amlan, (1961): *"Essays on Economic Development"*, Book Land Pvt. Ltd., Calcutta.

Entrepreneurship Development Institute of India, (1987): *"Developing New Entrepreneurs"* Ahmedabad, EDII.

Galbraith, J.R. (1969): *"The New Industrial Estates"*, Oxford and IBM Publishing Company, Calcutta.

Gangadhara Rao, N. (1973): *"Entrepreneurship and Growth of Enterprise in Industrlal Estates"*, Deep & Deep Publications, New Delhi.

Geoffrey G. Meredith, Robert E. Nelson, Philip A. Neck (1994) : *"The Practice of Entrepreneurship"* Sultan Chand & Sons, New Delhi.

Gupta, C.B. and Khanka, S.S. (1996): *"Entrepreneurship and Small Business Management"* Sultan Chand & Sons, New Delhi.

Gupta, C.B. and Srinivasan, N.P. (2001): *"Entrepreneurial Development"* Sultan Chand & Sons, New Delhi.

Joshi, Arun, Lala Shriram, (1975): *"A study in Entrepreneurship and Industrial Management"*, Orient Longman, New Delhi.

Killy, Peter (Ed.), (1971): *"Entrepreneurship and Economic Development"*, The Free Press, New York.

Khanka, S.S. (2002): *"Entrepreneurial Development"*, S. Chand & Company Ltd., New Delhi.

— — (1990): *"Entrepreneurship in Small Scale Industries"* Himalaya Publishing House, Mumbai.

Kumar, S. Ashok, (1990): *"Entrepreneurship in Small Industry"*, Discovery Publishing House, New Delhi.

Khursheed Ahmed Bhat (2000): "*Modern Small Scale Industries and Industrial Sickness*", Anmol Publications Pvt. Ltd., New Delhi.

Mali, D.D. and Bundopadhyay, R. (1993): "*Small Industry Development in North East India : Status and Strategy*", Omsons Publications, New Delhi.

Mali, D.D. and Deka, P. (1987): "*Industrial Development in North East India*", Omsons Publications, New Delhi.

Manohar U. Despande, (1982): "*Entrepreneurship of Small Scale Industries*", Deep and Deep Publications, New Delhi.

Mathur, B. Satish (1999): "*Sickness in Small Scale Sector*" Concept Publishing Company, New Delhi.

Nalini. V. Dave (1987): "*Industrial Sickness and Key Areas of Management*", Deep and Deep Publications, New Delhi.

Panda, R.K. & Meher, Raj Kishore (1992): "*Industrial Sickness: A Study of Small Scale Industries*", Ashish Publishing House, New Delhi.

Pieris, Ralph, (1969): "*Studies in Sociology of Development*", Rotterdam University Press.

Prasain, G.P. (2003): "*Entrepreneurship Development*", Sunmarg Publishers and Distributors, New Delhi.

— — (2006): "*Entrepreneurship and Small Scale Industries*", Akansha Publishing House, New Delhi.

Prasain, G.P. and Singh, Nixon E (2007): "*Entrepreneurship in Small Scale Industries in Manipur- A Case Study of Imphal East and West District*", Akansha Publishers, New Delhi.

Rao, N. Gangadhara, (1986): "*Entrepreneurship and Growth of Enterprise in Industrial Estates*", Deep and Deep Publications, New Delhi.

Rao, Subha P., (2001): "*Entrepreneurship and Small Business Management*", Discovery Publishing House, New Delhi.

Reddy, K.C. (1983): "*Sickness in Small Scale Industries*" Ashish Publishing House, New Delhi.

Ricardo, David, (1962): "*The Principles of Political Economy and Taxation*", London, J.M. Dent & Sons Ltd.

Say, J.B., (1827): "*Production, Distribution and Consumption of Wealth*", John Grigg No. 9, North Forth Street, Philadelphia.

Sahu, P.K. & Mishra, D.P (1992): "*The Critical Appraisal of Industrial Sickness*", Kanishka Publishing House, Delhi.

Schumpeter, J.A., (1949): "*The Theory of Economic Development*" Cambridge, Havard University Press, Massachussetts.

Sen, S.K., (1964): "*Studies in Industrial Policy and Development of India*", Progressive Publishers, Calcutta.

Sharma, K.L., (1967): "*Entrepreneurial Performance in Role Perspective*", Abhinav Publications, New Delhi.

Sharma, R.K. (1990): "*Industrial Entrepreneurship*", Kalyani Publishers, Ludhiana.

Simha, S.L.N. (Ed.) (1978): "*Industrial Sickness: Role of Banks,*" "Credit Management (Planning, Appraisal and Supervision)", Institute for Financial Management, Madras.

Srivastava, S.S. and Yadav, R.A (1986): "*Management and Monitoring of Industrial Sickness*", Concept Publishing Co., Pvt. Ltd., New Delhi.

Subhash Gangwal (1990): "*New Dimensions in Industrial Sickness*", Subline Publications, Jaipur.

Vepa Ram, K. (1980): "*Modern Small Scale Industries – Problems and Prospects*", Sage Publications, New Delhi.

B. Articles

Bhargava, R.K. (1972): "*Importance of Small Scale Industries*", Commerce (Supplement) 124 (3190), 24th June.

Bhat, R.S. (1974): "*Growth of Entrepreneurship in Small and Medium Sectors*", *Indian Journals of Public Administration,* Vol. XX. No. 3, July- September.

Bhat, A.R. (1972): "Development of Small Industries In Free India", *Commerce,* 125 (3196), 19th August.

Choudhury, R.P. (1973): "Changing Pattern of Small Business Finance in India", *Indian Journal of Commerce,* Sept.

Chandra, Poojary M. (1996): "Small Scale Sector : Myth and Reality", *Economic and Political Weekly,* Vol. XXXI, No. 21, May, 25.

Deolamkar, Viveks, (1987): "Financial Practices of Small Business in a Backward Region – Analytical Approach", *Indian Journal of Commerce,* Vol. XLI., Part 3, No. 152, July – Sept.

Gaikwad, V.R., and Tripathi, R.N. (1970): "Socio-Psychological Factors Influencing Industrial Entrepreneurship in Rural Areas", National Institute of Community Development, Hyderabad, May.

George Herbertan Evens Jr. (1949): "The Entrepreneur and Economic Theory", *American Economic Review.*

Himachalam, D., (2001): "Entrepreneurship Development Programme: Need for Revival", *Banking and Finance, January.*

Hazarika, Jatin, (1998): "National Seminar on Entrepreneurship Development – Keynote Address", *IIE Guwahati*, 10th December.

Hussain, Abid, (1998): "*Small Enterprises Protection*", *Laghu Udyog*, Vols. XXII & XXIII, Nos. 6 to 7, Jan. - Sept.

Indu, K.S., (1997): "*Infrastructure Development for the Small Scale and Tiny Units*", *Laghu Udyog*, Vols. XXI & XXII, Nos. 6 to 8, Jan.-Dec.

Joshi, Navinchandra (1995): "*Rejuvenating Small Industrial Sector*", Yojana, Vol. 9 No. 13.

Khan, Nawab Ali, (1984): "*Development of Small Scale Sector in India*", *Yojana*, Oct. 15.

Khanka, S.S. (2000): "*Development of Small Scale Industries in Assam*", *Journal of the North Eastern Council*, Shillong.

— — (2000): "*Making the Entrepreneurial Society- With reference to North East India*", National Seminar on Entrepreneurship Development, IIE, Guwahati.

Kaveri, V.S. (2000): "*Financing of Small Scale Industries : Issues and Suggestions*", *National Seminar on Entrepreneurship Development*, IIE, Guwahati.

Kaushik, K.C. (1997): "*50 years of Small Scale Industries in India – Policies and Programmes*", *Laghu Udyog*, Vol. XXI & XXXII. Nos. 6 to 8, January – Dec.

Lal, Sudarshan, (1974): "*What Do We Mean By Small Industries?*", *Yojana*, Vol. No. XVII Nos. 23 and 24, January.

Lingaraj, B.P. and Girikumar, T. (1982): "*Problems of Small Industries in a Developing Country*", *Decision*. Vol. IX, No. 4, October.

Maran, K. (2001):"*Role of SSIs in Growing Economy*", *Industrial Herald*, July.

Manalel, James, (1997): "*How Beautiful is Small*", *SEDME*, Vol. XXIV (4), No. 4 Dec.

Mali, D.D. (2005): "*Developing Entrepreneurship in North East – Experiences and Strategies*", Keynote Address, ICSSR Sponsored National Seminar on "*Entrepreneurship Development in Manipur*", Department of Commerce, Manipur University.

Mali, D.D. (1998): "*Area Approach on Entrepreneurship Development*", *National Seminar on Entrepreneurship Development*, IIE, Guwahati. Dec.

Mathem, P.M. (1997): "*Union Budget and Small Enterprises*", *Economic and Political Weekly*, Vol. XXXII, No. 14, April 5.

Nagayya, D. and Rao, K.V. (2000): "Small Scale Industries : Challenges and Strategies in the Liberalised Period", *SBI Monthly Review*, July.

Nagayya, D. and Appa Rao, P.B. (1998): "Perspective of Entrepreneurship Education and Training", *National Seminar on Entrepreneurship Development,* IIE, Guwahati, Dec.

Nagayya, D. (1998): "*Entrepreneurship Development : The North Eastern Region - Retrospect and Prospect*", *National Seminar on Entrepreneurship Development,* IE, Guwahati, Dec.

— — "*Data Base in Researchable Areas in the Small Enterprise Sector*", *National Seminar on Entrepreneurship Development,* IIE, Guwahati, Dec.

Nixon Singh E., Bijoykumar Singh E. (2002): "*Entrepreneurship in Manipur : Problems & Prospects*" Paper presented in the Vth *Annual Conference of North Eastern Economic Association,* Lala, Assam, Dec.

Papanek, G.F. (1962): "*The Development of Entrepreneurship*", *American Economic Review,* Vol. LLI May.

Prasain, G.P., Devi, Sancharita R.K. (1997): "*Women Traders in Manipur – A Case Study*", *The Indian Journal of Commerce,* Vol. L., No. 193, Part IV, Dec.

R. Shanmugham (1990) : "*Entrepreneurship in Small Scale Industry: A Case Study*", *Indian Management,* Vol. 29, Nos. 11 & 12, Nov. & Dec. 1990, pp. 13-15.

Reddy, B., Dasaradharami (2000): "*Financing of SSI Sector by Commercial Bank*", *Banking and Finance,* Vol. XIII, No. 12, Dec.

Saikia, S.K. (1992): "*Problems of Small Units in North Eastern Region*", *Yojana.* Vol. 36, Nos. 13-23, Nov. 30

Sahu, P.K. (1985): '*Some Conceptual Issues on Industrial Sickness.*" *Indian Journal of Commerce,* March, 1985, Vol. XXXVII, Part No. 142, p. 21

Singh, M.P. (1998) : "Growth and Development of SSI," *Laghu Udyog,* Vol. XXII to XXIII, Nos. 6 to 7, Jan. - Sept.

Singh, Biren, P. (2000): "*Role of DIC Thoubal in Rapid Industrialisation*" *Manipur Today* Vol. XX, No. 2 April, 23.

Singh, Tomba Kh. (2002): "*Industrial Sickness in Manipur – A Case Study of Small Scale Industries*", an unpublished Ph.D. Thesis submitted to Manipur University,

Srivastava, S.P. (1987): "*Institutional Finance for Small Industries*", *Indian Journal of Commerce,* Vol., XLI, Part 3, No. 152, July – Sept.

Singh, D.P. (1995): "*Marking Challenges in Small Scale Industries*", *Management Researcher,* Vol. 11, No. 12, July - Dec.

Vepa, Ram K. (1997): "*Small Can Be Beautiful – Recommendations on*

Small Enterprises", Economic and Political Weekly Vol. XXXII, No. 27, July 5.

C. Reports and Surveys

India, Ministry of Industry, Report of the Expert Committee on Small Enterprises, (Chairman: Abid Hussain), New Delhi, 1997.

Govt. of Manipur, Director of Commerce & Industries, Industrial Policy of Manipur, 2002.

Govt. of Manipur, Directorate of Economic & Statistics, Statistical Abstract of Manipur, 1998.

Govt. of Manipur, Directorate of Economic & Statistics, Statistical Abstract of Manipur, 2004.

Reserve Bank of India (RBI), "Compendium of Circulars on Small Scale Industries" (July 1978 – December 1999) Mumbai, March, 2000.

All Manipur Entrepreneurs' Association (AMEA), Economic Development Towards 2001 AD.

D. Journals and Periodicals

Laghu Udyog, Delhi
Indian Manger, New Delhi
Decision, Kolkata
Mainstream, Kolkata
Yojana, New Delhi
Productivity, New Delhi
Indian Journal of Commerce, New Delhi
Indian Journal of Entrepreneurship, Ahmedabad
Journal of Industry and Trade, Kolkata,
Kurushetra, New Delhi
Economic and Political Weekly, New Delhi
Chartered Accountant, New Delhi
Industrial Herald, Chennai
IBA Bulletin, Mumbai
Manipur Today, Imphal
Business Week, New York
Banking and Finance, Kolkata
Business India, Kolkata
Business Horizons, Bloomington

Business India, Kolkata
Business Horizons, Bloomington
Chartered Secretary, New Delhi
Indian Journal of Marketing, New Delhi
Vikalpa, Ahmedabad
Business World, New Delhi
Journal of Accounting and Finance, Jaipur
Margin, New Delhi
Prajnan, Pune
The Strategist, Kolkata
Kangleipak Business Review, Imphal.

Index